Redemption Songs

How Bob Marley's Nova Scotia Song Lights the Way Past Racism

Jon Tattrie

Pottersfield Press, Lawrencetown Beach, Nova Scotia, Canada

Library and Archives Canada Cataloguing in Publication

Tattrie, Jon, author
Redemption songs : how Bob Marley's Nova Scotia song lights the way past racism / Jon Tattrie.
ISBN 978-1-897426-87-6 (paperback)
1. Racism. 2. Marley, Bob. Redemption song. 3. Garvey, Marcus, 1887-1940. 4. Blacks--Nova Scotia--History. 5. Rastafari movement.
I. Title.
HT1521.T38 2016 305.8 C2016-902944-1

Cover design: Gail LeBlanc

Pottersfield Press acknowledges the financial support of the Government of Canada for our publishing activities. We acknowledge the support of the Canada Council for the Arts. We are pleased to work in partnership with the Province of Nova Scotia to develop and promote our creative industries for the benefit of all Nova Scotians.

Pottersfield Press
83 Leslie Road
East Lawrencetown, Nova Scotia, Canada, B2Z 1P8
Website: www.PottersfieldPress.com
To order, phone 1-800-NIMBUS9 (1-800-646-2879) www.nimbus.ns.ca

Printed in Canada

Conseil des arts du Canada Canada Council for the Arts
Funded by the Government of Canada Financé par le gouvernement du Canada
Canada NOVA SCOTIA

To the Hundingo Man, Eddie Carvery,
for inspiring this and so much more.

"We are going to emancipate ourselves from mental slavery because whilst others might free the body, none but ourselves can free the mind."

– Marcus Garvey
Sydney, Nova Scotia, 1937

Contents

Introduction

Listen:

Fifteen thousand Germans roar at the dark stage. Bob Marley and the Wailers had just ripped up the night with a sixty-minute set before ending with a drum-heavy take on "Exodus." Marley left with a wave. The dancers rhythmed off stage. The drummer departed with the bass and guitar players. The stage sat in black silence for three minutes.

The crowd wants more, hollering skyward, pleading with the reggae star to light the darkness again. In the summer of 1980, a generation removed from the Second World War, a half-generation before German reunification, the Dortmund, West Germany, crowd sounds like a jet engine begging for one more supernova from the dying star.

They erupt when a bass line burbles out of the darkness: "Marley! Marley! Marley!"

Marley's Rasta "Yeah!" emerges from the black, bringing back the light. "This song is called 'The pirates yes they rob I, sold I to the merchant ships,'" Marley says.

The singer stands alone under two spotlights, strumming his guitar and singing quietly. The simple acoustic song stands in sharp contrast to the heaving reggae set that preceded it. Lighters spark up over the darkened crowd.

"Won't you help to sing another song of freedom?" Marley asks.

They do, singing like children at his feet.

A strap breaks and the guitar falls. Marley stops singing. He speaks the next line, tapping on his sweat-covered forehead, flipping back his dreadlocks like a lion's mane. "Emancipate yourself from mental slavery," he says. "None but ourselves can free our minds."

He closes his eyes as a thick dread overlays his face. He throws his hair back like he's generating energy. He asks again, "Won't you help to sing another song of freedom?"

The band returns as Marley dances. He's the oldest thirty-six-year-old who ever lived.

"Redemption Song" is the last song on the last album Marley ever recorded. A year later, weeks before the cancer took him, it would become one of the last songs he ever sang.

Johnny Cash covered "Redemption Song." So did Bob Geldof, Jackson Browne, Stevie Wonder, and Rihanna. Alicia Keys sang it when Nelson Mandela died. U2's Bono carried its words in his pocket every time he met with a president or prime minister. Bono called it a prophetic utterance or, in the words of Marley, a small axe that could fell the big tree.

"Redemption Song" is one of the greatest hymns composed by humanity. And it was born in Nova Scotia.

★ ★ ★

"Redemption Song" seems like a personal reflection on death, or a song against slavery. Straightforward, right? Bob Marley is a black man singing that physical slavery is over, and that the next step is for black people to mentally free themselves from inner chains.

The only problem is that the traditional interpretation is totally wrong.

★ ★ ★

In this book, we'll follow the song's extraordinary journey from its birth in Nova Scotia to its afterlife lighting the way past racism and into a richer human future. We'll learn that racism is wrong because the very idea of race is wrong; it's witchcraft thinking.

People once genuinely believed in witches and murdered tens of thousands of people to stop the black magic. Then people still believed in witches, but decided it was wrong to kill them. Then people stopped believing in witches altogether, and killing them became a non sequitur. Eventually, the whole idea of witches died. Now, no one believes in witches. (At least not in the West.) It's even hard to believe that people ever genuinely believed in witches.

The same thing is happening to the belief in race.

★ ★ ★

To understand what Bob Marley is really saying, we're going to learn about scientists who are reading our DNA to discover the real truth about humans. We're going to journey back to the birthplace of humanity and meet Adam, the man who is father to us all, and Eve, everyone's mother. We're going to follow the exodus out of Ethiopia's Rift Valley and learn how one band of humans separated and evolved in different ways, creating what we now call the races. We're going to pay close attention to a later, secondary process – the invention of racism.

"Redemption Song" was born in Nova Scotia, so we'll set our story there. We'll learn how different races came to Nova Scotia, and how racism came a century later. We'll meet the man who discovered that black is beautiful, and finally best expressed himself on the eve of his own death by speaking these words in a hall in Cape Breton: "We are going to emancipate ourselves from mental slavery, because whilst others might free the body, none but ourselves can free the mind."

Redemption Songs will show us how those words reached Marley as he climbed his own Mount Nebo and saw the Promised Land spread out at his feet – a Promised Land Marley would see, but not enter. A Promised Land we can enter today.

Because Bob Marley wasn't only speaking as a black man singing to black people. He also spoke as a white man, and he sang to white people.

★ ★ ★

We'll start our story on the shores of Mi'kma'ki in the summer of 1605 as a wooden ship brings a crew of eclectic adventurers determined to create a new world.

Song 1:
The First Canadians

When a man and woman have sex, they mix up their genes to create a child that is like both parents, and yet utterly new. When two cultures embrace each other, a similar thing happens. But what about when it's a three-way?

★ ★ ★

One of the first three Canadians, Lusofonia, was born in a bustling trade town called Elmina in the British colony of the Gold Coast (today's Ghana) during the 1570s. He grew up in the multicultural, heavily fortified town of 20,000 people. The coastal enclave drew Portuguese businessmen and adventurers in for trade. Locals created a pidgin language to talk to them, and later turned it into a full Creole.

Lusofonia spoke that Creole, plus Portuguese, plus his own language, along with Dutch and several pidgins. Not surprisingly, he worked as a translator. The more languages Lusofonia knew, the higher a wage he could command.

Like his father, he worked as a *grumete* – a fixer who could translate, make arrangements, and help navigate your ship. Lusofonia learned European languages and customs from the *lancados*, or European men who had married local women and essentially become Africans.

Lusofonia stood out as a bright, ambitious young man up for any well-paying adventure. His mind easily straddled Africa and Europe, and he devoured stories about a whole new world opening up across the Ocean Sea, as he called our Atlantic Ocean. It's possible he had already visited the western shore of the Atlantic. At the least, he got a first-hand report from his uncle, who had visited the new world.

He deepened his knowledge by talking with indigenous people from the new world who had sailed to Europe and Africa – some as ambassadors, some as prisoners. The Mi'kmaq chief Messamouet, for example, travelled to France around 1580 to improve his French. Lusofonia either met Messamouet in Europe, or he met with another Mi'kmaq person in Africa. He learned about Mi'kma'ki, the fertile land now attracting the interest of both the British and French. He also learned some Mi'kmaq language. Many Mi'kmaq spoke Portuguese – learned to trade with the European fishermen working their coastline – and Lusofonia already spoke Portuguese.

By 1600, Lusofonia had made himself one of Elmina's most sought-after *grumetes*. The fixer grew famous under his adopted European name, Mathieu Da Costa.

In 1603, he caught the attention of a French adventurer named Samuel de Champlain.

★ ★ ★

Champlain, the second of three first Canadians, was born in Brouage, France, in 1574. It was a fortified, cosmopolitan port town on the west coast whose traders travelled the world. That ocean soon took him adventuring on behalf of King Henry IV. No one really understood why the provincial child had a special line to the king, but rumours were that Champlain was Henry's illegitimate son.

Champlain, a talented geographer and sailor, shared the enlightened vision of Henry's court. King Henry, Champlain, and many others were growing sick of the religious wars that had burned across Europe for centuries. Tens of thousands of people were murdered for their religious beliefs, and millions were displaced or forced to convert from one branch of Christianity to another. Champlain himself had to abandon the Protestant faith of his birth to survive as a Catholic. Henry, his possible father, famously declared, "Paris is worth a Mass" after converting to become King of France. Henry's court wondered: Could humans start a brand-new society on the other side of the Atlantic that would be free from the disease of intolerance?

Champlain sailed to Spain's American colonies in 1599 to find out, and spent two years watching in horror as Spanish conquistadors violently pacified South America, killing millions of indigenous people. Champlain left, disgusted with the Spanish approach. He hungered for a peaceful, happy world where different people could live together. While the Spanish saw the indigenous people as less than human, Champlain's Christianity led him to see them as children of the same God.

King Henry dreamed of building a new world in the land that would become Canada. Champlain fell in love with the idea of a broad-minded, tolerant culture founded on differing mindsets, rather than the European norm of different mindsets murdering each other until only one remained.

As 1603 approached, plans solidified. Champlain would lead an expedition to Acadia, where Pierre Dugua de Monts intended to establish a colony. Champlain, the mission's mapmaker, would decide where to plant the flag. His task was to form diplomatic relationships with the Mi'kmaq and found the colony. But Champlain needed a fixer who knew the Mi'kmaq people, who could speak their language, and who had the talent to help establish the new civilization. He hired Da Costa.

★ ★ ★

Membertou, the third original Canadian, was born in Kespukwitk District on the southwest coast of Mi'kma'ki in the early 1500s. The future grand chief was a district chief, married and with children, when he first saw a wooden sailboat haul itself over the horizon in 1534. It carried the French explorer Jacques Cartier, who mapped parts of the Mi'kma'ki coastline as he sought a shortcut to Asia. He also claimed it for France, but didn't share the news locally. Had he, Membertou might have let him know he wasn't in China.

Membertou learned more about these newcomers when his cousin, Messamouet, travelled to France and returned with knowledge of the languages and cultures of Europe. Membertou was a legendary leader even in his own day. Europeans especially took notice of him. First, there was that beard – he was perhaps the only Mi'kmaq man to sport one. And he was tall, much taller than other men, and his wellspring of dignity made him seem even taller.

As district chief, and later as the appointed grand chief of all Mi'kma'ki, he ruled not with power, but with persuasion and prophecy. He spoke gravely, and after much consideration. He knew how to guide disagreeing people into agreement.

Along with the political duties, he was a famous healer. He cured the sick through dance, chant, and ritual. His victories as a warrior created fresh legends for a culture already steeped in lore. He wrote songs, too.

By 1603, Membertou was the most famous and well-regarded human in Mi'kma'ki. According to Marc Lescarbot, he was nearing his legendary great age of one hundred. He sought out European visitors and dreamed up a great future for his people paired with these technologically advanced immigrants. Membertou saw that if he could strike an alliance with a nation like France, he could secure his people from their bitter rivals, the Passamaquoddy.

Much of the Mi'kmaq system of governance had been designed to limit warfare, and the culture revered restraint and dignity, shunning overt forms of aggression. Their ideal person freely gave to those in need, and offered generous hospitality to strangers.

Membertou wanted to further advance Mi'kmaq society.

All he needed was a European with a vision to match his own. That's when the ships emerged from the fog.

★ ★ ★

Champlain's mission to Acadia/Mi'kma'ki set out in 1604. But instead of working with the Mi'kmaq, they let fear get the better of them and the colonists settled on an island they called Île Saint Croix in today's Bay of Fundy. The mistake proved disastrous.

Champlain thought they'd be safe on the island and expected to paddle ashore for food. But winter froze the water into wobbly chunks of ice and the colonists couldn't get on or off the island. Scurvy and starvation set in. Settlers grew big "fungus flesh" in their mouths, which rotted their faces. Their teeth fell out and they could only take liquids. Their mouths bled, their bodies throbbed in pain, and their guts grinded them up. When it was done, forty of the seventy settlers were dead.

Champlain should have seen it coming. Actually, he did. "It was difficult to know that country without having wintered there. Winter came upon us sooner than we had expected," he wrote after the calamity. "There are six months of winter in that land."

The Passamaquoddy, Penobscot, Maliseet, and Mi'kmaq people living on the mainland overlooking the island watched in sad amazement.

★ ★ ★

The French settlement left the island in the spring of 1605 and moved to the mainland.

Da Costa, the translator and scout, quickly made friends through his language and cultural skills while Champlain laid out his plans. He and his remaining thirty settlers were the only Europeans north of Florida. They needed local allies to survive.

Champlain named their copse of houses Port Royal. Membertou lived near the new settlement and quickly impressed Champlain and Da Costa as an important ally, a person of great influence, and a major Mi'kmaq leader. He lived in a town, too, surrounded by high palisades, and knew deeply how to live year-round in Mi'kma'ki. One French missionary, Pierre Biar, described Membertou as "the greatest, most renowned and most formidable savage within memory of man: of a splendid physique, taller and larger-limbed than is usual among them, bearded like a Frenchman. [He has] a proper sense of dignity for his position as a commander."

Oh – can we forgive the use of "savage"? It's a sloppy translation of *sauvage*, which meant woods dweller.

Another French writer said the Mi'kmaq "were more humane and more honorable than many of those who bear the name of Christians."

Membertou dressed to affect people. When he first met the French, he sported a beautiful otter robe. He tooled around the coast in a fine European shallop decorated with Mi'kmaq totems. Membertou was a businessman, as well as a political, military, and religious leader. He knew Europeans well, and knew how a partnership could profit his people. He regularly sailed out to meet incoming French ships and traded with them at sea to avoid competition on the mainland.

★ ★ ★

We know Champlain thought highly of Da Costa by the princely sum he paid him for his services. Champlain understood his mission required someone who could speak to the Mi'kmaq and win their trust.

We know the European-African adventurers respected Membertou. And we know Membertou saw huge potential in the new arrivals. He took the name of the French king – the man who was likely Champlain's own father, remember – and called himself Henri Membertou.

Membertou extended immense hospitality to his guests, helping them find food and grow crops, teaching them about local politics, and even converting to their religion, Christianity.

Port Royal lived large that winter. They started the good-times club the Order of Good Cheer over the winter of 1606, and luxuriated in ample food and entertainment.

When funding ran dry and Champlain's crew had to leave in 1607, they left two French caretakers. Membertou, ever the good neighbour, stepped in to help. When the French returned in 1610, Port Royal was as good as new.

★ ★ ★

Notice something surprising? No one mentions that Da Costa is black, or Champlain is white, or that Membertou is red (Remember when that used to be an acceptable way to describe a First Nations person?). That's because they weren't. Da Costa was African, Champlain was European, and Membertou was Mi'kmaq.

If the Order of Good Cheer owned a bigger budget, they could have brought over a performance of the new smash hit dominating London's stages: *Othello*, by William Shakespeare. Othello, famously, is a black-skinned Moor. But the play obsesses over the *Moor* part – Othello being culturally adrift in Europe, not racially disadvantaged.

It's like they hadn't heard of race. And maybe they hadn't.

We'll see in Song 12 and Song 13 that someone had to invent race before someone else could invent racism – but first we need to jump ahead from the winter dreaming of Membertou, Champlain, and Da Costa to learn how a King was born a slave.

Song 2:
A King in Chains, Part 1

Jaycee Lee Dugard's happy young life ended when a man grabbed her off the street of South Lake Tahoe, California, as the eleven-year-old walked to school on June 10, 1991. Her abductor brutally beat her and locked her up. Three years later, she gave birth to a daughter. A second daughter came in 1997. Dugard believed she would be held in captivity for the rest of her life, and that her daughters were likewise born into slavery.

So what should she tell them? Would it be better to teach them she was born free, snatched, and held against her will? No. Her children were beautiful and flooded her with hope. She decided to keep those horrors from them. When freedom came, her children were fifteen and eleven – the youngest was the same age as her mother was at the time of the abduction. Stepping out of their captor's control in 2009, they learned they had been slaves.

* * *

Boston King's father faced a similar decision, but chose to tell his children the truth about their situation. Mr. King – we don't know his first name, or birth last name, just the name his son Boston got in captivity – was born at home and grew up with his family in Africa. We don't know where in Africa

One day in the mid-1700s, Mr. King was out walking when he was abducted and shipped to South Carolina to be a slave. He married a woman in the same predicament, but we don't know her name.

Mr. and Mrs. King had a son, and called him Boston King. Mr. King turned to religion, finding strength in prayers and song. He rose early to spend time with his family before going to toil for his captor.

At the end of a Sunday, he stepped into the woods for a moment of private prayer. He returned and told his son about Africa, and how they were being held against their wills – but he also said they were "beloved by his master."

He died when his son was still a boy. "To the utmost of his power he endeavoured to make his family happy, and his death was a very great loss to us all," his son later wrote.

Boston King doesn't give many details about his mother, but like Jaycee Lee Dugard, her main concern was the well-being of her children. She made natural remedies from what scant supplies they had to help them when they got sick, sewed them clothing, and kept them hopeful.

Boston King's captors put him to work at age six, and by twelve he was working hard in the fields. One day, the boy slave had a vision that changed his heart. "At mid-day, when the cattle went under the shade of the trees, I dreamt that the world was on fire, and that I saw the supreme Judge descend on his great white throne. I saw millions of millions of souls; some of whom ascended up to heaven, while others were rejected and fell into the greatest confusion and despair," he writes.

The dream stunned him. He stopped swearing and keeping bad company, resolving to serve God as best he could. He started thinking about freedom.

★ ★ ★

The vision didn't protect him. The boy lost his master's boot not long after the dream, so the man confiscated King's shoes and forced him to go barefoot all winter. At sixteen, he was rented to another man, who used him to run his shop. King screwed up one day. "My master beat me severely, striking me upon the head, or any other part, without mercy," he tells us.

Once, when his captor left the house for the evening, robbers broke in and ransacked the place. King was terrified – but not by the robbers. "When I came in the evening and saw what had happened, my consternation was inconceivable, as all that we had in the world could not make good the loss," he said of the danger he faced with the other slaves.

His captor beat him most of the way to death, leaving him bedridden for two weeks. Around the same time, the American Revolutionary War broke out. King guarded little things like nails, which had become rare. He got blamed for another theft and was "beat and tortured most cruelly." This time, his injuries sidelined him for three weeks.

He knew he had to escape. No one was going to rescue him.

★ ★ ★

One day King's captor let him ride his horse to carry out some of his duties, but another slave took the horse from him. King knew his master would beat him again. As American rebels fought British soldiers, King saw his chance for freedom.

"To escape his cruelty, I determined to go to Charlestown [Charleston] and throw myself into the hands of the English. They received me readily and I began to feel the happiness of liberty, of which I knew nothing before," he writes.

It was the summer, late 1770s. King was about seventeen, and on his own. He'd run for freedom, but had to leave everything behind. He became ill and fell near death. "In this situation I was seized with the smallpox and suffered great hardships; for all the Blacks affected with the disease were ordered to be carried a mile from the camp, lest the soldiers should be infected and disabled from marching. We lay sometimes a whole day without anything to eat or drink."

Amazingly, King met an old friend, and his buddy nursed him to health. But the English soldiers had marched on, fleeing the advancing Americans. King fled, too, running after the English. He turned his smallpox into a weapon, using it to scare off people who meant him harm. The disease killed more people than every soldier in the Revolutionary War, but King survived.

He got a break when the English army sent wagons back to recover sick people who'd fallen behind.

King caught a ride and joined the retreating army. He found himself living in cottage number 25, near the hospital, and soon recovered. He marched on to Chamblem, South Carolina, and sought protection from Lord Charles Cornwallis, the top English military commander. (Don't confuse Lord Cornwallis with his uncle, Edward Cornwallis, who had founded Halifax in 1749.)

King stayed with the Cornwallis camp for three weeks and learned how to fight a war. The English needed soldiers, and found that offering freedom to American slaves was a win-win. It caused problems for Americans in their own territory and increased the number of English fighters.

The friend who saved King when he suffered from smallpox was wounded; King stayed at his side for six weeks while he recovered. King was "rejoicing that it was in my power to return him the kindness he had shewed." King fled onward another thirty-five miles to another base, where he stayed two months.

One afternoon, on orders from his captain, King went fishing, then returned to the camp. "To my great astonishment, I found all the English were gone and had left only a few militia. I felt my mind greatly alarmed, but Captain Lewes, who commanded the militia, said: 'You need not be uneasy, for you will see your regiment before 7 o'clock tonight.'" Calmed, King marched with the militia to rejoin the main army as it retreated from American soldiers.

The captain asked King to become his servant; King rebuked him, as he served a Captain Grey. Lewes told him Grey and all the others were likely American prisoners now, so King should recast his lot. "These words roused my indignation and I said some sharp things to him. But he calmly replied, 'If you do not behave well, I will put you in irons, and give you a dozen stripes every morning.'"

King obeyed his new master.

Lewes had stolen fifty horses from his own army and stashed them on an island. He sent King to retrieve the animals in the morning. Lewes rode off with the horses, leaving his slave behind. King decided to escape again. King fled that night, walking twenty-four hours before stopping at a farmer's house. The farmer showed unexpected kindness and let King rest up.

At a nearby river, he found more English soldiers and eventually rejoined Captain Grey. King told him that Lewes had deserted the army. Grey burned Lewes's house down and reclaimed their horses, but Lewes got away.

★ ★ ★

King was tasked with taking a letter to another band of English soldiers still in American territory. It was a dangerous mission, but King dove in.

He set off on foot at 3 p.m. and dodged the enemy, "whom I well knew would shew me no mercy." He passed safely through rebel territory and came within six miles of safety – and then the Americans arrived. King dove into the dirt and pressed himself face down until they passed without detecting him.

"I then arose, and praised the Name of the Lord for his great mercy, and again pursued my journey," he says. He found a tavern, whose owner blew out the candles at his approach and hid. King convinced the owner he was a loyal British subject and learned the Americans had passed by an hour earlier and would soon return. King rode with the tavern keeper to the British army. "[The captain] received me with great kindness and expressed his approbation of my courage and conduct in this dangerous business."

King was paid in shillings and promises. He used the money to reach Charleston and boarded a ship sailing for Chesapeake Bay. King sought work. He became a general servant, but earned so little he wore through his clothes and could not replace them.

He worked for several deadbeat masters before marrying a woman called Violet. King promptly got sick and was laid up for five weeks. When he recovered he sailed on, eight days this time, and the crew ran out of food. Starving, they were captured by an American whaling boat. King boarded the new vessel and the crew fed him en route to Brunswick, North Carolina.

The British still held slaves, and despite the British promises of freedom he feared being abducted again. "My mind was sorely distressed at the thought of being again reduced to slavery and separated from my wife and family, and at the same time it was exceedingly difficult to escape from my bondage because the river … was above a mile over," he says. He prayed to God for one more deliverance in exchange for his lifelong service.

★ ★ ★

King visited a friend in jail. The man had also been held as a slave and escaped, but he got caught and dragged behind a horse back to the prison. He was locked into the stocks night and day. The sight terrified King, as he knew the same fate could wreck him.

King enjoyed some freedoms, but he still basically lived as a slave. "And what is better than all, many of the masters send their slaves to school at night, that they may learn to read Scriptures. This is a privilege indeed. But alas, all these enjoyments could not satisfy me without liberty!"

King wrestled in his heart: did God intend for him to be a slave? Or did God intend for him to redeem himself into freedom? He decided to escape north.

His wife and family stayed behind, perhaps hoping to join him one day.

* * *

He used his little free time smartly. Now in New Jersey, he noted the rise and fall of the Raritan River that blocked his escape, observed the movements of the guards posted to stop prisoners and slaves from leaving rebel territory to get into British-held New York. King prayed all night, thinking the Lord had heard his cry, and would deliver him.

At one a.m., King crept from his bed, slipped down to the riverside and, like Saint Paul before him, found the guards miraculously asleep. He entered the river and waded to the distant shore. In the murky night, sentinels only half-imagined they saw a man crossing the river, and decided not to shoot, lest they draw attention to their negligence. King emerged from the water and fell to his knees praising God. He walked on until the sun rose, and then hid all day, travelling through bush and marsh, never on the road, to stay free.

He boarded one more boat and sailed into New York a free man.

★ ★ ★

His New York friends greeted Boston King like a king. To see him restored to liberty lightened their hearts and motivated everyone to praise the Almighty. "But notwithstanding this great deliverance, and the promises I had made to serve God, yet my good resolutions soon vanished away like the morning dew," King wrote. "The love of this world extinguished my good desires."

The war ended in American victory in 1783. European and North Americans descended from Europeans celebrated the "universal joy" of peace and freedom. But no freedom for people born in Africa, or to Africans. "Us, who had escaped from slavery, in number 2,000, were to be delivered up to their masters," King grimly writes.

After a few years of freedom, it seemed the English would betray the former slaves and send them back as "property" to the Americans. "This dreadful rumour filled us all with inexpressible anguish and terror."

Cruel men grabbed people off the streets and hauled them back south to slavery. Women were snatched out of their beds. The survivors fled outside. You could see them if you looked: the hungry, unsleeping men and women wandering the streets, holding their children tightly, eyes darting everywhere for coming danger.

The English found mercy and declared that all slaves should be free or freed if they had taken refuge behind British lines. The Treaty of Paris promised the British would exit "with all convenient speed, and without causing any destruction or carrying away any Negroes or other property of the American Inhabitants." George Washington, the American military leader and later president, interpreted this to mean American "property" such as Boston King should be returned, but British commander Sir Guy Carleton believed it meant slaves freed before the treaty would remain free. "Each of us received a certificate from the commanding officer at New York which dispelled all our fears and filled us with joy and gratitude," King says.

The Americans would soon regain control of New York and so the city was evacuated. Few African-descended people risked staying in a city about to fall under the control of a country that put Africans in chains. The British, and their slaves, fled to Canada (still called British North America in those days).

Boston King was free again. He started to run again.

Song 3: Prisoners

On the morning of August 14, 1970, police officers in Palo Alto, California, falsely arrested nine students and handed them over to a fake prison in a basement at Stanford University. They were locked up and controlled by nine other students who had been given fake prison guard uniforms (including mirror sunglasses) and real wooden batons. The guards strip-searched the prisoners, sprayed them to kill lice, and told them to put on a plain smock and cap. The guards attached a chain to the prisoners' feet to prevent them from getting away.

The prisoners were locked up. The guards started working eight-hour shifts in the jail.

Things deteriorated quickly. The guards began waking the prisoners in the middle of the night. They bullied the prisoners. Guards told prisoners to do push-ups as punishment for breaking rules or showing attitude. One student took to stepping on the backs of the other students as they did push-ups. He made other prisoners sit on the backs of prisoners and told the bottom student to do push-ups.

The next day the students/prisoners tore off their caps and numbers and locked themselves into the cells. They taunted the students/guards now unable to reach them. The night shift left, wearing the contempt of the day shift, who thought they'd lost control of the fake prison.

The day shift called in three more guards to get control of the prison. Heavily reinforced, the guards physically attacked the prisoners by spraying carbon dioxide from a fire extinguisher into the cells. The guards forced their way in, hauled out the prisoners, and ripped off their clothes. The prison leaders were shoved into solitary confinement.

The guards created a special-privilege cell where obedient prisoners reaped rewards such as getting dressed, brushing their teeth, and cleaning their faces. They got better food, too. The prisoners stopped seeing themselves as a unit, and began competing for access to the privilege cell.

The guards randomly swapped prisoners in and out of the privilege cell, thoroughly confusing them and making it clear that all power – including the power to decide what was good and what was evil – rested solely with the guards.

The guards, who were usually outnumbered three to one by prisoners, felt safer when they dominated the prisoners, and feared losing that domination. They enforced it even in petty ways, such as whimsically deciding if prisoners could go use the toilet or not. When they couldn't, the young men pooped and peed into a bucket, and soon the prison reeked like a dirty barn.

The students/prisoners and the students/guards came to think the roles had been decided by size, with the bigger men becoming guards and the smaller men becoming prisoners. Actually, the men were equal in size. But the guards looked bigger.

A day and a half into this created hell, one prisoner cracked. Sobbing and raging, he experienced emotional chaos and a sense of helplessness. He told the other prisoners, "You can't leave. You can't quit." A second prisoner started screaming and raging.

Rumours swept through the guards: the prisoners were planning an escape. The guards sought real police reinforcements, moved the prisoners into seclusion, and dismantled the basement prison. The prison break turned out to be a lie, and the angry guards forced prisoners to repeatedly clean toilet bowls with their bare hands and do push-ups and jumping jacks for hours.

Another prisoner collapsed mentally, sobbing into the arms of a real priest. The guards mocked him. Prisoners and guards chanted, "Prisoner 819 did a bad thing."

Prisoner 819 wept. He ran back into the prison to prove he wasn't a bad prisoner. He wanted to be a good prisoner.

If you randomly select ordinary people and put them in an evil place, most will act evilly. Ordinary people randomly selected to benefit from the evil will reap those benefits, and ordinary people randomly selected to suffer will reap that suffering.

★ ★ ★

By the fifth day, the guards had sorted themselves into different approaches. The tough-but-fair guards followed the rules scrupulously. The good guys broke the rules to do little favours for obedient prisoners. The third group grew meaner and arbitrarily punished prisoners, enjoying their humiliation.

Some prisoners rebelled and the guards broke their rebellions. Other prisoners broke mentally and endured whatever degradation came their way. Some tried to be super-slaves, obeying each command and trying to win favour from the guards.

A new student was arrested and tossed into the jail. Disgusted by what his fellow students were doing in a pretend prison, he refused to play along. He went on a hunger strike. The guards marched him into solitary confinement. Fresh from the outside and well aware that the power imbalance was arbitrary and phony, he continued his hunger strike and demanded he be released.

The other prisoners hated him. A guard said if any prisoner gave up his blanket, they'd release the disobedient prisoner. No one gave up their blanket. The disobedient prisoner spent another hungry night alone.

The guards grew more sadistic and often sexualized the punishments. The prisoners shrank into pathological inner prisons. The guards tied bags over their heads, chained their legs together, and force-marched the prisoners to the toilets.

Christina Maslach, a retired professor at the university, saw this display and said it was terrible. She was the first person – guard, prisoner, professor, observer – to state the obvious. Everyone had consented to this psychology test, but it had gotten out of hand.

The Stanford Prison Experiment ended that same day, six days into a planned two-week simulation.

★ ★ ★

Six days in a fake prison run as a university psychology experiment radically altered the behaviour of people selected to be in power or powerless. Everyone knew it was fake and had signed consent forms to act as prisoners or guards. Anyone could have left. Guards could have skipped their shifts. But no one did. The students pretending to be prisoners quickly became prisoners. The students pretending to be guards quickly became guards.

One baffled young man assigned to be a guard later said he thought he was incapable of such behaviour. The mock guard surprised and dismayed himself by learning he could be so cruel and brutal. He'd never dreamed of abusing people before. He didn't regret it at the time.

He felt horrified after the experiment ended. He realized that a nasty prison guard evidently lived below his regular identity. The mock prisoners learned that a servile inmate hid in their own psychological basements.

What would happen if you started a Stanford Prison Experiment and ran it for four hundred years? What if each generation of guard children was taught they were naturally superior and destined to be guards? And what if generation after generation of prisoner children was taught they were fated to always be prisoners?

Song 4:
A King in Chains, Part 2

Boston King's ship from New York docked on the southwest coast of Nova Scotia in August 1783. He headed to his assigned plot in the new settlement of Birchtown and, like all the other African refugees, cleared some land and built a simple hut before the winter came.

King, like lots of other people, lived in a dirt hole with a wooden roof for that first winter.

A lot of people died.

★ ★ ★

Some early Nova Scotians achieved incredible things despite the growing discrimination against people with African roots.

Barbary Cuffy worked as a midwife and had two children with her husband Stephen Cuffy in the 1760s. He died. Cuffy, with her children Deborah and Isaac, planted the freedom flag. She bought five hundred acres of land in Liverpool in 1764, becoming one of the first women to own land in Nova Scotia. Because she owned land, she could vote in town meetings. Centuries would pass before another woman or black person voted in Nova Scotia.

Cuffy sold some of her land in 1765 and 1769, before slipping off the pages. One source says Cuffy "returned to Plymouth" after 1787. Perhaps she had republican sympathies, or returned to family. Her son Isaac seems to have taken over some of her land and by 1811, locals still called it "Barbary's lot" or, as merchant and diarist Simeon Perkins called it, "my Barbary field."

★ ★ ★

As spring 1784 broke the grip of winter, Birchtown emerged as the biggest free black settlement outside of Africa. Its 1,500 people dug into the poor soil and fought for survival. The nearby white community of Shelburne had 17,000 residents, making it the fourth biggest city in North America.

Both communities hugged the same coastline that Mathieu Da Costa sailed along 180 years earlier. Birchtown had poorer land than Shelburne, and poorer access to fishing. The men and women, mostly people who had freed themselves, grew food and struggled through the seasons.

Violet King made her own unrecorded journey to Nova Scotia and joined her husband in Birchtown. She met Moses Wilkinson, a freed slave who was blind and lame, and a life-stirring minister. He set hearts afire at the Brother Moses Chapel, a Methodist congregation. Violet fell to the ground and cried for mercy. Christians raced to find Boston King who never set foot in the chapel. "At first I was much displeased and refused to go, but presently my mind relented and I went to the house," he writes. "I was struck with astonishment at the sight of her agony."

For six days Violet King lived in a spiritual trance. Then, God spoke peace to her soul and filled her with divine consolation. She walked in the light of God for nine months, before the dark parts of her heart spread and (King tells us) Violet fell again, this time to bad tempers and a great darkness of distress. This backsliding crushed her, and she took to her bed for eighteen months.

"However, the Lord was pleased to sanctify her afflictions and to deliver her from all her fears. He brought her out of the horrible pit and set her soul at perfect liberty," King says.

Violet King became luminous once more and the light of God radiated from her happy spirit. She spoke the word of God, and many followed her. Others made fun of her.

Violet prayed with a white man called Freeborn Garrettson, who had come to Birchtown to help with the church. He once owned African people, but underwent a mental emancipation a decade earlier when, aged twenty-three, he set them all free.

Boston King felt his own sin weighing heavily on him, keeping him up at night. He went to Joseph Brown, a former slave who had travelled with King on *L'Abondance* from New York to Nova Scotia and become a preacher.

"The more he spoke to me, the more my distress increased; and when he went to prayer, I found myself burdened with a load too heavy for me to bear," King writes.

He walked home through a little woods and kneeled to pray, but every time he tried, terror filled his heart, the earth seemed to move, and his hair stood straight up. Scared, King ran home. He kept away from the religious revival. He sank deeper into darkness and misery. He felt unworthy of living with the God-loving people of Birchtown and took himself into the forest to live with the other animals.

Winter was back, and so King slogged through waist-high snow. He started a campfire and shivered under one blanket. "In this lonely situation, I frequently entreated the Lord for mercy."

During good moments, he felt himself moving toward God. But more often his unbelief drove him in a different direction. "The devil persuaded me that I was the most miserable creature upon the face of the earth and that I was predestined to be damned before the foundation of the world," he confesses. "My anguish was so great that when night appeared, I dreaded it as much as the grave."

King lived in the woods for one year. Others started joining the hermit for night and morning prayers. In January, one of the outcasts read the Parable of the Sower, where seeds cast on inhospitable ground die, while those cast on fertile ground grow a hundredfold.

"The word came with power to my heart," King says. He saw himself as stony ground, with the word of God bouncing off him unfruitfully. "I was astonished that the Lord had borne with me so long."

King knelt in the deep snow and begged God to

free him. "That I might never find rest or peace again, 'til I found peace with him."

King, alone under sparkling winter stars, felt himself convert to God's way. But as soon as he returned to Birtchtown, he returned to his old ways.

King never tells us what was so wrong with him.

In March, he started hearing voices. They said, "Peace be unto thee." He decided to stay on his knees until he found that peace. Eventually, he had a vision of Christ in heaven. "I loved every living creature upon the face of the earth and I could truly say I was now becoming a new creature. All tormenting and slavish fear, and all the guilt and weight of sin were done away," he writes. King rose, unlocked his door, and rejoined his brothers and sisters in the church.

But six weeks later, his belief faltered. "Then the enemy pursued his advantage and insulted me with his cruel upbraidings: 'What will become of all your joy that you spoke of a few days ago? You see, there is nothing in it.'"

* * *

Everything we know about Boston King comes from the book he wrote. *The Methodist Magazine* published *Memoirs of the Life of Boston King, a Black Preacher*, in 1798. It's called a slave narrative, which was a popular type of writing at the time.

Anti-slavery activists sought out these narratives and published them to condemn slavery. The autobiographies were used to show that slavery was wrong, to show how Christian redemption played a crucial role in freeing people, and to show that progress was possible.

Books like King's were supposed to show that Europeans could end African slavery without it ending in murder and mayhem as black people sought revenge on their white oppressors.

That's probably why he doesn't write about the race wars between African Birchtown and European Shelburne in 1784.

★ ★ ★

Those who found it too hard to scrape a living out of rocky Birchtown walked over to Shelburne to seek work. They always got paid less than white people. The only ones who resented this more than black Birchtowners were poor white Shelburners, who now couldn't find work at all.

These pockets of European-African settlements in Nova Scotia were islands in a war zone between the Mi'kmaq and the British government. The Mi'kmaq controlled much of the land, but were regularly pushed back.

Benjamin Marston, Shelburne's chief surveyor, kept a diary recording the increasing hostility between white and black people. Marston, a white man educated at Harvard University, could see that the arbitrary and unfair distribution of land created conditions for trouble. He often shared his thoughts with Stephen Blucke, a great leader among the black population, who approved of his work.

Things really kicked off over the preaching of David George. Like King, his parents were abducted in Africa and brought to America, and he freed himself and moved to Birchtown. As a child, he'd seen his eight sisters and brothers whipped to the edge of death, hunted by horses and dogs, and saw his brother hung naked from a cherry tree. George was tortured, too.

He suffered a deep trauma when he had to watch his European "master" whip his mother until she stopped twitching. "I believe she was on her deathbed when I got off, but I have never heard since," he recalled in later years.

He started preaching in the very early days of Birchtown. "Numbers of my own colour were there, but I found that white people were against me I began to sing the first night in the woods at a camp, for there were no houses then built, they were just clearing and preparing to erect a town," he says.

"We had a meeting now every evening, and those poor creatures who had never heard the Gospel before were listening to me very attentively. But the white people, the justices, and all were in an uproar and said that I might go out into the woods, for I should not stay there."

But even race relations aren't black and white. George met a white man he'd known in the south, and that white man gave him land to build a hut church.

Things probably would have gone quietly if George had kept his message to African ears, but he regularly preached to Europeans, too. He converted William Taylor and his wife, both Londoners, and soon oversaw a thriving African-European congregation. "The Christians were all alive, and we had a little heaven together," George says.

But then he baptized Deborah Holmes, a white woman, and her family tried to abduct her out of the church. Holmes fought them off and tried to enter the lake to be baptized. Her sister grabbed her hair and dragged her out. Ultimately, her family was forced to let her make her own choice, and Holmes asked George to baptize her.

The idea of an African man – a former black slave – blessing a white woman enraged some European Nova Scotians. An armed mob of white men tied ropes to George's house and pulled it apart. The demolition crew swelled to a few hundred people and hauled down as many African homes as they could. The mob beat up the residents and chased them out of Shelburne.

The mob then turned on Benjamin Marston, Shelburne's chief surveyor, and hatched a plan to kill him as punishment for letting Africans settle on decent land. Marston fled to Halifax.

The mob, now fortified by some off-duty British soldiers, zeroed in on David George. He ran at full tilt and leapt into a swamp to hide. The mob yanked him out and beat him until he stopped moving. When he came to, he fled to Birchtown.

The Shelburne mob vented their fury for days, beating lone black travellers and attacking Birchtown itself, smashing apart houses and terrifying children. After a month, British troops marched from Halifax to restore order. The British governor, an ambitious Irishmen named John Parr, expressed frustration at the collapse of lawful rule. He gave full control of the area to a European-only council.

Pretty much every African person left for Birchtown. David George's Shelburne church was converted into a pub. "The old Negro wanted to make a heaven of this place, but I'll make a hell of it," the new owner liked to joke.

★ ★ ★

Famine swept through Birchtown, Halifax Annapolis, and Digby. Destitute people sold their best clothes for a few more days of food. White, black, or Mi'kmaq, everyone got hungry. "When they had parted with all their clothes, even their blankets, several of them fell down dead in the street through hunger. Some killed and ate their dogs and cats. Poverty and distress prevailed on every side, so that to my great grief I was obliged to leave Birchtown," King writes.

Unemployed and, after the riots, likely unemployable, King formed an ambitious plan to go to his father's homeland. It started on January 20 1787, when he met a Captain Selex, who hired him to make a chest. Delighted, King worked hard all night and built the chest. He walked through thick snow the next day and delivered the goods. But Selex rejected it, and ordered another. King staggered home, collapsing repeatedly from hunger. He expected to die that day, but kept moving. He and his wife were down to their last pint of cornmeal. Two killers raced to take the Kings – starvation and exposure.

But King built one more chest and this time Captain Selex approved. He paid King with food. "I was exceedingly thankful to procure a reprieve from the dreadful anguish of perish by famine," he writes.

That same year, God told King: "I will send, by whom I will send."

He took that to mean he should migrate to Africa and bring Christianity. "Especially when I considered that we who had the happiness of being brought up in a Christian land, where the Gospel is preached, were, notwithstanding our great privileges, involved in gross darkness and wickedness," he writes.

As he arranged the exodus to Africa, King spent his final Nova Scotia years worshiping the New Light. The Christian movement focused on the liberty of individual conscience and scorned structured religion. The New Light movement birthed the African Baptist Church in Nova Scotia, which will play a crucial role in drawing the electrifying Marcus Garvey to the province centuries later to deliver his landmark mental emancipation speech.

Other Africans in Nova Scotia used their freedom to sell themselves back into slavery to avoid death. They could offer themselves as indentured servants for five or six years at a stretch. Many poor European Nova Scotians did the same thing, pitting the two groups against each other in competition for scraps.

"The circumstances of white inhabitants were likewise very distressing, owing to their great imprudence in building large houses and striving to excel one another in this piece of vanity," King writes unsympathetically. "Had they been wise enough at first to have turned their attention to the fishery, instead of fine houses, the place would soon have been in a flourishing condition; whereas it was reduced in short time to a heap of ruins."

★ ★ ★

Boston King almost died before he could complete the circle to Africa. To get a bit of money and food, he joined a June 1788 fishing expedition to the Gulf of St. Lawrence, but a day-long storm nearly drowned everyone on board. A second ship, carrying food and supplies, vanished into the following fog.

The captain of King's ship swore a blue streak and stormed the deck in a rage.

His behaviour lit the lamp on painful memories for King, who had suffered a traumatic childhood of vicious, random beatings from an unhinged master. "I was stupefied like a drunken man and knew not what I was doing," King recalls. "My soul was exceedingly grieved at his ungodly language. I repented that I ever entered into his service."

King was a new, mentally liberated man, though, and told the captain his attitude would earn him a spot in the lake that burns "with fire and brimstone." The man listened to King in silence, and then cursed in his face. The captain egged the whole crew on, and King plugged his ears against the unholy tide.

* * *

In early 1791, King's religious work took him to Preston, a big black settlement a long walk east of Dartmouth. He preached with William Black, a Methodist evangelist travelling around Nova Scotia without pay. On good days in Preston, King preached to thirty-four people – all black apart from one white family.

"Sometimes I had a tolerable congregation, but alas I preached a whole year in that place without seeing any fruit of my labour," King writes.

In January 1792, a particularly bad sermon led

him into a familiar depression. He ramped up his preaching, tapping into a divine mood. He gained one more Christian, a success that buoyed his spirits. He preached to black people comfortably, but felt shame when white people turned up to hear the word of God. He felt ignorant and unable to teach them, assuming they possessed superior education. But he met with them, got to know a Mr. Ferguson, and King learned his own simple, honest style drew some white people to him.

Later that month, King finally got an opportunity to sail across the Atlantic Ocean to Freetown, Sierra Leone. John Clarkson, a famous white abolitionist who volunteered for the Sierra Leone Company in Nova Scotia, recruited black settlers for the new city and escorted them to Africa.

Each free black man was promised twenty acres, with another ten acres for their wives. Clarkson recruited 1,196 Nova Scotians and hired fifteen ships. He left with this first exodus from Halifax in January, offering "free" passage to Africa, which would be repaid in work on arrival.

On January 16, 1792, King sailed to Africa, reversing the journey forced on his father. The voyage nearly ended in disaster during a sixteen-day storm that scattered the fifteen ships. One man was washed overboard. King stood on deck with the man during the storm and saw him drown. Violet King got deathly seasick. "I expected her to die before we could reach land and had an unaccountable aversion to [burying] her in the sea," he writes. He prayed to God to spare her life until they reached land. Violet bloomed into perfect health.

The couple landed in Sierra Leone on March 6, and Violet quickly caught a putrid fever. After intense prayer, she again recovered. But it was fleeting; days later, amid loud rejoicing, she "expired in a rapture of love."

Malaria killed the Nova Scotian settlers so rapidly that it was hard to bury them all. Some eight hundred of the eleven hundred settlers got the disease; all but one of the one hundred white company employees also were hit. One out of every ten Nova Scotians relocated to Africa died of malaria that season. For the white Nova Scotians relocated to Africa, it was worse: fifty-seven out of the one hundred died.

King built himself a small hut and once more started a new life. He preached in the shade of a large tree.

★ ★ ★

One final word from Boston King. He travelled to England before returning to spend his last years in Sierra Leone. He'd turned a corner in his thinking, and reached a conclusion that we'll see Bob Marley advance two hundred years later. "I am now fully convinced that many of these white people, instead of being enemies and oppressors of us poor Blacks, are our friends, and deliverers from slavery, as far as their ability and circumstances will admit," he concludes.

He felt Christianity's ancient message held the key. The white Methodists treated him as a brother in Christ, not an enemy in race. "I did not believe there were upon the face of the earth a people so friendly and human as I have proved them to be," he muses.

★ ★ ★

Now we have many of the needed ingredients for our *Redemption Songs*. We see the human road leading from Africa to America to Nova Scotia, and back to Africa. We see the sparks of divinity that can liberate human minds.

We need an ambitious man to unite those scattered religious communities. Get ready to meet the whirlwind known as Galloping Richard Preston.

Song 5:
The Bystander Effect

In January 2014, a Quebec man stumbled over a yellow warning line in a Montreal Metro station, fell onto the platform, and started bleeding profusely. For sixteen minutes, he bled out as dozens of people stood by. He died shortly after paramedics arrived to treat him. The coroner blamed "the indifference of the passengers."

"It says a lot about citizen apathy in our society. There is not much positive to write about this operation," he concluded.

In 2011, a woman collapsed on stone stairs on a busy London street. She lay flat out and motionless. A man sat on a wall a metre away and continued to read his newspaper. Dozens of people walked by, sometimes glancing at her as she suffered. Her hand twitched and her mouth lolled open.

No one helped her.

The thirty-four strangers who passed her had

formed a temporary social agreement: this woman was outside of society and no one need help her. No one need get involved. Sociologists call it the Bystander Effect.

Finally, a construction worker arrived and broke the group consensus by asking the prone woman if she was okay. Others then rushed in to help. They learned they were unknowingly participating in a psychological experiment and that the woman was an actress.

In the early 1970s, a woman sat in a small hotel room filling out a form with a group of strangers. Smoke billowed into the room. The hotel was on fire. For twenty minutes, she sat in silence, because all the strangers saw the smoke and did nothing. She soon learned she, too, was in a psychological experiment demonstrating the hypnotic power of the Bystander Effect.

Humans, especially those raised in Western traditions, see ourselves as individuals. Our default setting is to seek individual causes, and assign individual blames. We hold individuals to account for their own actions. But human brains are very old social organisms. Like ants and bees, we often act in unison, driven by dimly understood social movements.

"It's always very distressing to watch situations like this where people are obviously suffering and no one's actually helping them," says Helen Haste, a psychology professor at the University of Bath. "What we have here are two conflicting rules.

"One is the rule that we ought to help. And the other is that we ought to do what everyone else is doing. Here you have a group of strangers who are exerting the pressure not to intervene, not to help, and it's very difficult to rebel."

Once the trance of the Bystander Effect is broken, people do rush in to help. But they first need a free-thinking person to race in and break the spell.

Song 6: Galloping Richard Preston

Galloping Richard Preston was one such person. He burst through Nova Scotia's Bystander Effect with his free-thinking rebel mind.

He entered the world as a slave on a Virginia plantation in 1791, around the time Boston King got to thinking about returning to his father's land. Richard's mother taught him he was free in God's eyes. She told him slavery was a sin and just plain wrong. But the sin entered the master, not the slave. Richard should not burn with shame as a slave. She burdened him with earning his own freedom.

As a young man, he stood six feet one inch tall, showed a history of mixed race in his face, could read and write, and, more importantly for us, could stir souls with his oratory. His mother fled America during the War of 1812 and went to Canada.

Richard stayed back. He worked and saved and in 1816, at twenty-five, emancipated himself from physical slavery through manumission (he bought himself). Sometime after his mother left, he mounted his horse and went looking for her. How big could Canada be?

Richard sailed to Halifax and learned his mother lived in a nearby African community. He found her free and happy in Preston. Whatever name he was born with, he dropped it then and there and declared himself to now be Richard Preston.

Preston apprenticed himself to John Burton, a former Methodist missionary who now headed the Baptists in the Halifax area. Burton's European-Nova Scotia standing seemed to give him a lock on the post as preacher to African Nova Scotians. His flock would be driven out of any white church, and the church leader needed white approval.

In 1823, Preston was a licensed minister forming a plan to unite the scattered African diaspora.

"By 1824, Preston was appealing to the bonding sentiments that were the cement of slave society in an attempt to coalesce the black congregations around his leadership. From rural area to rural area, the news of Preston spread, followed by his authoritarian presence and his exhortations," his entry in *Dictionary of Canadian Biography* (*DCB*) records.

The difference between having a freeborn white man preach to you and having a slave-born, self-emancipated black man preach is significant. Many Africans, and some Europeans, picked Preston. More joined him when the Anglican Church split over the question of black congregants and a popular movement tried to drive Africans out of the Anglican Church.

Preston travelled to England to be ordained in Liverpool in 1831. Like King – and soon, like Garvey and like Marley – he encountered a different world in England. It was dominated by white people, but the social movement of the day was abolitionist. Preston listened eagerly to the forceful oratory of white leaders such as William Wilberforce and Thomas Fowell Buxton speaking against slavery.

In May 1832, Preston became an ordained minister. By June, he pulled a packed house to his London chapel, with people filling the pews and standing areas and spilling outside. He thrilled the Christians by making it obvious that slavery was cruel and evil.

He soon sailed back to Nova Scotia ready to preach – and also having raised £600, an impressive display of his talents for church-building. "The issue of emancipation burned stronger in his heart than ever before," the *DCB* says.

On April 14, 1832, his fellow Christians had founded the African Chapel on Cornwallis Street, one of the first black-run organizations in the province.

Many European-Nova Scotians held bad ideas about African-Nova Scotians, imagining them born stupider and deserving of a lower citizenship. Preston's confidence, good looks, charm, and intelligence challenged that perception.

The church opened a school. Other Nova Scotians rallied to his call, both white and black, men and women. With them, Preston created the African Abolitionist Society, one of Nova Scotia's earliest and greatest movements. In it, many Nova Scotians crossed racial, cultural, and national boundaries to shout from the rooftops about the cruelties of slavery, and make it plain to all people that it must end.

* * *

From its founding day, Halifax bought and sold humans in the Grand Parade. In 1750, ten per cent of Halifax's population of a few thousand had African roots, and four hundred were held in slavery. In Halifax also lived seventeen free Africans.

Black people built the city streets, cutting Halifax out of the Mi'kma'ki woods. Many free or freed people worked as labourers, stevedores, and builders. Fortifying Citadel Hill, they helped defend the nascent settlement from Mi'kmaq and French attacks.

Some of these people are rumoured to have settled in the northern part of the city in a community that would, decades later, be called Africa-ville, or Africville. This community will play an important role in birthing "Redemption Song."

* * *

In 1854, Preston started a new, more local movement: the African Baptist Association. It united the Baptist churches and soon united Nova Scotia's scattered black communities. Always bold, Preston sought a collective voice to address spiritual matters, but also social and financial matters. He spread the Baptist faith and built a common African-Nova Scotian identity.

On horseback, Preston galloped and trotted the dusty roads of Nova Scotia, riding into towns with a mixture of devotion and humour that earned him the love of many people. In the 1840s, he and his followers rode into the Dartmouth Lake Church, swelling the church's regular congregation. A bigger mob grew, too, drawn to drive him out. Inside the church, hearing the menacing growl of dozens of angry men set against them, Preston spoke to his people. "We'll go outside. As the Grace of God gives me sufficient power over men and devils, I fear neither," he said.

He led his people safely out of that confrontation. He did the same thing in the First Preston Church. One day when everyone was deep in prayer, the front door blasted open and a hostile gang of men poured into the sanctuary.

Preston kept right on praying.

He raised one calm eyelid and looked at the mob. "Are you looking for Satan?" he asked. "Never mind looking for him, I'll tell you when he's coming."

Boom.

★ ★ ★

Richard Preston spent the next two decades galloping across Nova Scotia to share his liberating vision. He died on July 16, 1861. His grief-stricken friends, family, and fellow Christians filled the Cornwallis Street church, sitting in all of its pews, standing in its aisles, and straining to listen to his funeral from the streets.

"The bishop is gone," someone cried. "He's crossed the flood to glory; protect him, Jesus!"

"A prince, a great man, has fallen in Israel," mourned Reverend Benson Smithers. "The founder of our churches, Father Richard Preston, is dead.

"Yes! He was a great leader. Now it is time to bury him."

The Reverend Henry Jackson spoke about the

far side of freedom. After the hard struggle so many of the gathered had made to free themselves from physical slavery came the greater battle: to emancipate themselves from mental slavery.

Jackson told the mourners, "His ideals and thoughts will survive him. Can you remember him saying, 'Listen! Listen! At present we are a poor people. We have been so recently snatched from the cruel grasp of slavery and its concomitant degradations that we have so little to be proud of, compared to others.

"'Our change of life, of soil, of climate, the substitution of a moral life for heretofore mere physical responsibilities, was so sudden and complete that it will take many years for us to readjust. But readjust we must. The time will come when slavery will just be one of our many travails.

"'Our children and their children's children will mature to become indifferent toward climate, and indifferent toward race. Then we will desire, nay, we will demand to be able to obtain our fair share of wealth, status, and prestige, including political power. Our time will have come, and we will be ready. We must be.'"

Galloping Richard Preston shattered the Bystander Effect's hold on thousands of people.

We need a prophet to see what these now-united people can do.

Song 7:
Colouring Humans

Adolf Hitler served as the environment minister for India's Nationalist Congress Party before losing his Meghalaya seat in February 2003. He once explained to a reporter that yes, another Adolf Hitler was "at one point in time" the most hated man on Earth, but as his own full name was Adolf Lu Hitler Rangsa Marak, no one should have a problem.

Hitler was an Aryan, of course, and that gifted him a life at the top of India's caste system. The other Hitler imagined he was an Aryan, too, but we'll explain that later.

India has five colours of people and uses the caste system to rank them according to their value. Here are the four "varnas," plus the people so lowly they don't get an official ranking:

Brahmins sit at the top. They get the best spots in life and take jobs as religious and secular teachers.

Kshatriyas come next, and they get jobs in public service, administration, maintaining law and order, and defence.

Vaishyas handle commercial activity in the business sector.

Shudras land at the bottom of the official list and get stuck with semi-skilled or unskilled labour.

Dalits live below the caste system and are better known in English as the untouchables. They have to do things like remove animal corpses from the road, clean toilets, and labour on farms.

Roughly speaking, Dalits are the darkest people and Brahmins are the lightest. The word "varna" comes from Sanskrit and literally means colour. It's probably related to the English word "varnish" as both come from the same root language, Proto-Indo European.

Many historians think the colour-based ranking system comes from the Aryans who arrived in India about 3,800 years ago and started to take control, forcing other people to accept ranks beneath theirs. That's why Adolf Hitler kept sending research missions to India. The European Adolf Hitler, that is.

Jamaica, meanwhile, has three colours of humans: white, brown, and black. During colonial times, it was more complicated.

Here we go: The child of a white man and a black woman was a mulatto; a mulatto person's and a black person's baby was a sambo; a mulatto person and a white person made a quadroon person; a quadroon person and a white person had a mustee; if a mustee person and a white person have a kid, she's a musteefino, and a musteefino is essentially a white person.

Got it?

But back to the three primary human colours in Jamaica: white, brown, and black. Generally, white people were the British ruling class and their modern-day descendants, and they usually got the best jobs and nicest lives. They got to set the cultural standards for beauty, too, and so spread the word that the lighter the skin, the hotter the person. There aren't many white people in Jamaica.

Brown people are the children of white and black people, and generally take the second tier of life. They have straighter hair, too. Along with the white people, they total less than 10 per cent of the population.

Black people can trace their ancestors back to Africa quite directly, and most of their ancestors arrived in Jamaica after being abducted in Africa. That accounts for about 90 per cent of all the humans on the island. (I don't know what colour the Taino were, but Jamaica's first settlers were killed off completely soon after Europeans arrived in the 1500s, ending 3,500 years of a human history.)

Canada has two colours of people: white and black. Generally, white people are the European settlers and their modern-day descendants; they usually got the best jobs and nicest lives. They got to set the cultural standards for beauty, too, and so spread the word that the lighter the skin, the hotter the person. White people make up about 84 per cent of Canada's population.

Black people make up less than 10 per cent, and often come from people like Boston King and Galloping Richard Preston, or explorers like Mathieu Da Costa.

For a long time, Canada also had red people, but this now sounds ancient and offensive. First Nations people have yet to be assigned a new colour.

* * *

In 1936, Nova Scotia's tourism department helpfully broke down the province's human population into five races so visitors wouldn't be alarmed at the variance. A handsome collection of portraits printed on the back of a guidebook outlined the five Native Types of Nova Scotia, as mentioned in Ian McKay and Robin Bates' 2010 book, *In the Province of History: The Making of the Public Past in 20th-Century Nova Scotia*.

The five races are English, Scotch, French Acadian, Irish, and Hanoverian. A modern reader might look at the fisherman, fiddler, knitter, and Highland soldier and say: Those are all white people. And the government agrees, describing them as "five distinct white races." Perhaps this passage will inspire a sultry novel called *Fifty Shades of White*.

A Mi'kmaq reader would perhaps wonder if she should be described as a non-Native Type. African Nova Scotians are firmly ignored.

In the decades since that brochure ran, most of us have amalgamated our racial taxonomy of white people down to one category. If we had to add a geographic element, it'd be European (leaving aside the many non-white people who migrated to Europe over the centuries). Let's look at an example of mind-expansion right here in Nova Scotia to see how people recategorize each other from Us versus Them, to just Us.

* * *

As we saw in Song 1, in the early 1600s Catholic French settlers arrived in New France, called Mi'kma'ki "Acadia," and started farming. They built on the friendship of Champlain and Membertou and lived for 150 years in peace, interrupted by the occasional violent spillover from European wars.

In 1749, Edward Cornwallis founded Halifax, recruited waves of Foreign Protestants (my ancestors among them) from across Europe to settle his Nova Scotia, and they soon numbered enough to start replacing the Acadian farmers.

In 1755, Cornwallis's successor, Charles Lawrence, drove the French settlers out of the province in a violent, bloody campaign called *Le Grand Dérangement* or The Expulsion. Few other Nova Scotians cared, and many (including my ancestors) soon moved into the now-vacant farmland. And for the next one hundred years, The Expulsion was distinctly a non-Nova Scotian event. It does not appear in the proto-tourism pamphlets.

But then a strange thing happened. An American poet named Henry Wadsworth Longfellow held a dinner party in 1840 and enjoyed a guest's second-hand tale about a young Acadian woman separated from her beau during the expulsion from Grand Pré. Inspired, the poet got to work and seven years later published *Evangeline: A Tale of Acadie*.

Longfellow was a best-selling poet, in a day when such creatures existed, and the poem was a big hit. It landed on the school curriculum and millions of American teenagers wept over "the forest primeval, the murmuring pines and the hemlocks" and "listed" to the mournful tale of love in Acadie, "home of the happy."

Those Americans grew up and took holidays in Nova Scotia to see the forest primeval. It did not exist. Longfellow never came here, and wrote from imagination; Evangeline never existed, and was birthed from that same imagination. So the government set about building the forest primeval and the heart-severed Evangeline.

"Entrepreneurs developed a formidable infrastructure around this brand, complete with advertising copy, postcards, railway coaches, steamships, and pseudo-events," write McKay and Bates. "With only a slight exaggeration, one could acclaim the 19th century Land of Evangeline as the very early beginnings of the 20th century theme park."

I've been to Grand Pré many times. Its fertile meadows, weeping willows, and romantic statue of Evangeline in front of a replica church beat solidly at the heart of Nova Scotia. We take visitors here, and bring our children. A poem turned a largely forgotten historic event into an abiding presence of dispossessed people. Longfellow and his coach-loads of American tourists transformed Acadians from an Other to an Us. Today, most Nova Scotians experience the Acadian story as part of their own broader identity, even if their genetic roots fought on the expelling side.

So it seems plausible that we could expand our taxonomy once more, and encompass our collective African-Nova Scotian history into mainstream identity.

★ ★ ★

Foreigners tend to have a hard time spotting the difference within India's colour coding, and African visitors to North America may wonder why black people are usually brown, and brown people are Indians, but they're not Indian like American Indians.

To outsiders, colouring humans seems bonkers. But if you're born inside a colour-coded system, the difference is as clear as black and white.

Song 8:
Climbing the Bottomless Pit

Some thirty years after Galloping Richard Preston entered into the earth, a young Marcus Garvey found himself trying to climb out of it.

His father had brought him into the hole and then removed the ladder. Marcus had no idea where his father had gone, or how he was going to get himself out of the deep hole they had dug.

Father and son were building a vault for a wealthy client. The two spent hours side by side digging deep into the earth. At lunchtime, Mr. Garvey had climbed out on a ladder – and then pulled the ladder up, abandoning his son in the bottom of the pit. Marcus spent hours crying for rescue, then fell asleep, dreaming of a dead man peering down at him. His father eventually returned and called the incident a lesson in defeating fear.

His father's name was Malchus Garvey, but it seems everyone (including his wife) called him Mr.

Garvey. A proud, self-educated man who had been born a slave, Mr. Garvey gathered books in his home to ensure his children would rise further than he.

He had seen the physical emancipation of his people; he hoped his son would see the mental emancipation. As a boy, Marcus often snuck into his father's library to learn. By age seven, he played priest to the other children, creating his own divine service, complete with songs and prayers, and entrancing the boys and girls with his passionate sermons.

From a young age, he also worked for his father.

Garvey later described his father this way: "My father was a man of brilliant intellect and dashing courage. He was unafraid of consequences. He took human chances in the course of life, as most bold men do, and failed at the close of his career."

Prophetic words from the Rasta prophet.

★ ★ ★

Malchus Garvey was born into slavery in Jamaica. He lived through the generation of emancipation, so his son Marcus was born free on August 17, 1887, in St. Ann's Bay. His wife, Sarah, came from peasant farmers.

The house Marcus grew up in overlooked the former home of an Anglican minister who had fought emancipation. The minister believed African-Jamaicans should naturally be held as slaves to the benefit of lighter-skinned people like himself.

As a teenager, Marcus landed an apprenticeship with the man who used to own his father, and who likely expected to own Marcus. Marcus worked a hard forty-hour week for free. Marcus had a broad, flat nose, dark skin, and curly hair.

That appearance meant a lot in a Jamaica earthquaked apart along tri-racial lines. Of the one million people on the island, 800,000 were African-Jamaican descendants of the humans captured in Africa and brought across the ocean to be worked as slaves. About 15,000 inhabitants were brown, or mixed-race. The tiny 5,000 population of European-descendants where white, and they ruled the island. Browns might visit with whites, but neither white nor brown sought the company of black. Some reformers hoped the island would be re-stratified so that talent determined who rose to the top and who fell to the bottom, but on the day Marcus Garvey was born, his black status cast him to the bottom of the pit.

⋆ ⋆ ⋆

Garvey had a close childhood friend in the daughter of a local minister. At fourteen, she abruptly announced her father was moving her to Scotland, telling her "she was never to write or try to get in touch with me, for I was a 'nigger,'" Garvey wrote.

The girl was white; Garvey saw for the first time that that was important.

His childhood friend Isaac Rose describes a young Garvey who had started working in printing. "Marcus Garvey was a fellow like this: all the time when I meet him, he wear a jacket and every time, his two jacket pockets full of paper. [He was always] reading and telling us things that happened all over the world. Him know I don't know, but him telling us. He was very interested in world affairs."

In 1905, Garvey moved to Kingston, the capital

of Jamaica, to start a career in printing. He stood five feet seven inches and possessed an energetic, stocky body. His eyes X-rayed people as he spoke. He impressed his boss at P.A. Benjamin Manufacturing and soon became the first black man to hold the post of foreman. Every preceding foreman had been English.

When the print workers went out on strike in 1908 to fight for better wages and working conditions, Garvey dropped his tools and joined them in a leading role. At age twenty, he showed skill for organizing people behind a common cause. The employers broke the strike after a few weeks and fired Garvey, along with most of the other leaders.

Garvey likely knew this could happen and accepted the rupture of a promising career for the deeper values. "The politics of my country disgusted me," he wrote. "I started to take an interest in the politics of my country and then I saw the injustice done to my race because it was black, and I became dissatisfied on that account."

He took to the streets, pushing political pamphlets into the hands of workers enjoying a rum-fuelled night out at Victoria Pier. In 1910, he won an election to be first assistant secretary of the National Club, Jamaica's first nationalist political party. An older member described the winning impression Garvey made: "He carried a pocket dictionary with him and said he studied three or four words daily, and in his room, he would write a paragraph or two using these words."

He soon printed the club's journal, *Our Own*. His role in the party earned him a mention in the *Jamaica Times* newspaper for a "sedulous pamphlet" about politics.

Garvey took elocution lessons from Robert J. Love to turn his country accent into a more refined voice. Love was famous for oratorical skills that could gather him an audience and drive them in what direction he chose. He described himself as "decidedly black" and fought hard for social reform. Love, in his journal *Jamaica Advocate*, argued for a Pan-African idealism that planted a Back to Africa seed in Garvey's fertile mind.

Garvey tested his new skills by entering public speaking competitions.

★ ★ ★

Garvey soon created a journal of his own, immodestly called *Garvey's Watchman*, in 1910. It lasted for three years, advocating for helping the poor. Also in 1910, the ambitious Garvey, still only twenty-two, invested all of his money into a trip to Costa Rica aboard a steamship. He intended to work as a timekeeper on a banana plantation.

He stepped onto a humid, hot island reeking of rotten bananas and riven by industrial strife between the poor Jamaican labourers and the prosperous North American managers. The sides clashed over a planned 12 per cent wage cut. Garvey quickly had to choose between those who paid him and his fellow Jamaicans suffering hardship. He watched as managers bullied and insulted the workers.

In the spring of 1911, he started another new journal called *Nation*. The pugnacious paper quickly bloodied the noses of rival journals and thrilled many poor workers. A critic sneered that Garvey wrote the "scurrilities of a vile penny-a-liner."

Garvey slammed into everyone who didn't measure up to his moral standards. When a fire destroyed West Indian-owned businesses in Limon, Garvey's paper suggested the fire brigade focused on saving the home of a wealthy white Jamaican and ran out of water. Police grabbed Garvey and assaulted him, hoping to punch him into submission.

They didn't break him. Unfortunately, his printing press did break. United Fruit owned all of the replacement parts and ignored his requests for repair. He stopped publishing for a time and focused on casual labour to support himself. He travelled through Panama, Honduras, Ecuador, Colombia, and Venezuela, including a stint at the new Panama Canal. Garvey talked to the ordinary poor, recording their stories.

American contractors paid white workers in gold and black workers in silver. Disgusted and in poor health caused by the jungle weather, Garvey returned to Jamaica in 1911. His homeland exploded into a nationwide strike as he stepped off the ship in Kingston.

In early 1912, Garvey happened upon a scene of rioting men attacking the white governor of Jamaica, a man named Sydney Olivier. Angry workers threw stones and rocks at Olivier, hitting him in the head with a brick. Garvey's usual instincts to stand with the poor were overturned by a desire to protect the attacked, and he shielded the governor with his own body and guided him to safety.

★ ★ ★

Garvey, like many colonial subjects of the time, grew up thinking the British must be the most amazing people ever to live on Earth. At age twenty-five, he wanted "to find out if it was different there," and sailed to England in 1912. London acted as the great engine of an empire not yet smashed by the coming Great War.

He had read newspaper accounts of a racially progressive country where, unlike the racial prison of North America, humans were judged by the content of their character, not the colour of their skin. He came to learn. No universities yet operated in the West Indies, and his savings could not have covered a European tuition. But he could benefit from the libraries of London.

"When we visited England, we found a different state of affairs. We ourselves, who are not coloured but black, found no difficulty in securing lodgings," he wrote.

Garvey studied books, but also people. He watched the British parliamentarians attack each other in sharp debates at the House of Commons, and watched ordinary orators try to stir the people from Speaker's Corner in Hyde Park. Garvey, never lacking courage, stepped onto the box himself and tested his skills in a foreign land. His African roots set him apart from all other speakers and drew a curious crowd. Some of his misty admiration and veneration of England reflected back to him from the minds of many Londoners, who likely imagined this dark-skinned man was a visiting dignitary from the outer empire. Black people were such a minority in London that to Londoners they seemed individual curiosities, rather than an ethnic group.

As he learned, Garvey earned his living working on the London dockyards. But his irrepressible drive soon took him to work that better suited his ambitions. He found a job in the small media empire of Duse Mohamed Ali, the Egyptian owner of *African Times and Oriental Review*, columnist for *New Age*, and producer of great plays.

Ali had organized the Universal Races Congress in London in 1911. Diverse racial ideas flew across the stages and minds. Should the races be arranged hierarchically? What benefits did mixed races bring? Could mixed marriages save the West Indies by giving it a population that bridged the black-white divide?

Garvey saw the ad for black writers in the *African Times and Oriental Review*, walked into the office, and remained there until they gave him work as a handyman and message runner. Here he learned about the Pan-African movement that would soon dominate his thinking.

He re-established contact with Sir Sydney Olivier, whom he had recently saved in his post as governor of Jamaica, and who was now back in England working for the Board of Agriculture. From there, Garvey built a network of high-level contacts.

Ali, a black man, writer, public speaker, and master communicator, taught Garvey many skills. Garvey pushed himself into the journalistic side of the magazine, writing "The British West Indies in the Mirror of Civilization," his take on European greed eating its way through his homeland.

He specifically blasted the colonial government for allowing race to define people back in Jamaica.

The colonial government tried to be progressive by colour-blind recruiting to the civil service, but cancelled the pilot project after a surge of black men took them up on the offer and started running the colony.

The civil service returned to a system that preferred whites by using nominations, and then nominating only people with European DNA. "The service has long been recruiting from an inferior class of sycophantic weaklings whose brains are exhausted by dissipation and vice before they reach the age of thirty-five," Garvey wrote. "The people [of the West Indies] will be the instruments of uniting a scattered race who, before the close of many centuries, will found an Empire on which the sun shall shine as ceaselessly as it shines on the Empire of the North today." This stirring vision won him followers and backers in England and in the U.S. It built bridges among the African diaspora, offering a common cause for a scattered people.

Garvey devoured ideas and found a way to attend law classes at Birkbeck College. He listened carefully to Ali's business plans to take over white-dominated sectors like banking and shipping.

★ ★ ★

Garvey saved his money and funded a Grand Tour of Europe's great cities. He started on the night train north to Glasgow, Scotland, then Paris, Monte Carlo, Boulogne, and Madrid. He began travelling with missionaries.

"I have seen wonders. At some places, I have been the only black man seen for a good time. Some of the tourists are wondering how a black man can travel about so much; some take me for an African millionaire," he wrote to a friend in Jamaica.

Ever curious, he befriended fellow travellers and locals, expanding his knowledge of how people thought and acted. At one point, he made a connection that must have astonished his friends back home. "I am engaged to a Spanish-Irish heiress whom I had the pleasure of meeting on the Continent," he wrote. His heart's desire flew against his mind's disapproval for mixed-race couples. "It is somewhat destructive of my principle, yet I hardly think I can change my mind in marrying her."

Despite the lofty engagement, he returned to London broke and needed money to get back to Jamaica. He earned it through freelance writing and spent his spare time reading in the British Museum, studying the black history that had been kept from him. "I read [Booker T. Washington's] *Up From Slavery* and then my doom – if I may so call it – of being a race leader dawned on me."

In June 1914, he sailed back to Jamaica, hundreds of ideas and dozens of destinies racing through his mind. In the cramped confines of third-class passage, he wrote mind-expanding essays designed to free others like he had been freed.

"Sons and daughters of Africa, I ask to you arise, take on the toga of race pride, and throw off the brand of ignominy which has kept you back for so many centuries. Dash asunder the petty prejudices within your own fold; set at defiance the designation of 'nigger' uttered even by yourselves, and be a Negro in the light of the Pharaohs of Egypt, Simons of Cyrene, Hannibals of Carthage, L'Ouvertures and Dessalines of Hayti … who have made, and are making, history for the race," he wrote.

He rejected any idea of downplaying his black skin and African features and called on others to do the same. Many felt shame at having even "one drop" of black blood in their heritage, but Garvey flipped that insult into a source of pride. "Once the African blood courses through the veins, you belong to the company of Negroes."

★ ★ ★

Garvey travelled widely in his twenties, across South America, the Caribbean, and Europe, but he had not yet set foot in Africa.

In Jamaica, he once struck up a conversation with a missionary from the West Indies on his return from Basutoland (today's Lesotho) with his Basuto wife. It painted a "horrible and pitiable" image of Africans in slave-like conditions, toiling under European- or American-controlled companies and governments.

"Where is the black man's government? Where is his president, his country, his ambassador, his army? I could not find them," Garvey wrote.

His emancipating mind leapt into a future where existed a "new world of black men, not peons, serfs, dogs and slaves, but a nation of sturdy men making their impress upon civilization and causing a new light to dawn upon the human race."

The ideas he had collected in his mental and physical travels began to coalesce into a prophetic vision as he lay in bed on the slow-moving ship home. Still an unknown man with little money, power, or institutional backing, he dreamed beyond his shadow of a global movement uniting the African diaspora.

But he stepped back into Jamaica alone, and made his own way to his new accommodation in Kingston. Five days later, he became chief recruiting officer for the organization he hoped would turn his heavenly dream into earthly reality: the Universal Negro Improvement Association and African Communities (Imperial) League, or UNIA. Its mission was "to establish a brotherhood among the black race, to promote a spirit of race pride, to reclaim the fallen and to assist in civilizing the backward tribes of Africa."

Its motto: "One Aim! One God! One Destiny!"

★ ★ ★

He drew inspiration from Gold Coast (now Ghana) lawyer J.E. Casely Hayford's novel *Ethiopia Unbound: Studies in Race Emancipation*. Ethiopia often represented Africa itself in such writings. Garvey, the poor son of an abducted African, dedicated his life's work to the liberation of the black race.

He started with words. He rejected the idea that "Negro" was a shameful word and embraced it as his own identity. He shocked brown people (and probably any white people paying attention to such things) by sneering at them and their belief that the lighter the skin, the better the person. A black man was expected to try and move "up" toward white, not "down" to black. Garvey sought to overturn that world view: "The prejudice in these countries is far different from that of America. Here we have to face the prejudice of the hypocritical white men who nevertheless are our friends [and] also to fight down the prejudice of our race in shade colour," he wrote.

The Gleaner eventually noted his return from London, after he sent them a press release. He dropped the names of the high and mighty he had met to push himself into the newspaper, but then spurned them for his black brothers and sisters. "I had to decide whether to please my friends and be one of the 'black-whites' of Jamaica and be reasonably prosperous, or come out openly and defend and help improve and protect the integrity of the black millions and suffer."

As always, he leapt off the train for the footpath below.

* * *

By July 1914, he had recruited enough UNIA members to hold a meeting and elect officers. They named him president of the UNIA.

Amy Ashwood soon joined. The seventeen-year-old quickly moved the UNIA headquarters out of Garvey's hotel room and into a big house rented in Kingston. People described the teenager as a brilliant intellectual with a mischievous sense of humour. Garvey's ideas found a kindred spirit in Ashwood, who embraced her black skin as he did his own, and who also dreamed of race emancipation. Unfortunately, Garvey was still engaged to that Spanish-Irish heiress.

* * *

When the Great War erupted, Garvey wrote a letter to King George V. "Being mindful of the great protecting and civilizing influence of the English nation … and their justice to all men, especially their

Negro subjects, we hereby beg to express our loyalty and devotion to His Majesty," he wrote.

Garvey lit the boosters under the UNIA and soon it was rocketing up the social skies to draw the approval of the mayor of Kingston, business leaders, philanthropists, and even Governor Sir William Manning, who sent his support and money.

Garvey supported himself by selling greeting cards and tombstones. In 1915, Garvey broke off the engagement to the European heiress, telling her, "Marriage between us is now impossible. You will be far happier with a member of your own race; so will I be with one of mine. I have seen a girl, blood of my blood and of my own race."

He became engaged to Ashwood. "Your Napoleon is longing to see you, longing to gaze into your beautiful eyes," he wrote to Amy. "Let no mother, no father, no sister, no brother, stand in the way of the redemption of Africa. I will always worship at your shrine."

★ ★ ★

Before leaving his native Jamaica in 1916 to find his destiny on the global stage, Marcus Garvey issued a prophecy.

"Look to Africa for the crowning of a Black King," he told his followers. He added a passage from the book of Psalms: "Ethiopia shall soon stretch out her hands unto God."

When his vision came true fourteen years later and Haile Selassie was crowned emperor of Ethiopia, some of Garvey's followers would come to see him as a John the Baptist witnessing the new Jesus Christ on Earth. His words would become sacred, and would found Rastafarianism. Bob Marley would convert to Rastafarianism, read Garvey's 1937 Nova Scotia speech, and write "Redemption Song."

Garvey would disavow his own prophecy as soon as it came true. His followers would break into two groups: Garveyites, who would listen to the man, and Rastafarians, who would use Garvey to go beyond Garvey.

Our prophet has his vision and he's setting out on a journey that will twist and turn before improbably delivering him to Sydney, Nova Scotia, to make his landmark speech about mental emancipation.

While he sails from Jamaica, let's move some mountains and meet Nova Scotia's Black Highlanders.

Song 9:
Moving Mountains

In 1936, Nova Scotia moved the Highlands 425 miles from Yarmouth to Cape Breton.

Premier Angus L. Macdonald, a romantic figure deeply attached to his Highland Scottish roots, had decided that the province should better celebrate its Scottish history. For the last two hundred years, Nova Scotia mostly identified itself as a modern British outpost on the far side of the Atlantic. Macdonald thought it should embrace the roots of its Latin name, New Scotland.

So he decided that the Highland name should leave the Yarmouth hills and attach itself to Cape Breton's mountains. He helped establish the Cape Breton Highlands National Park of Canada, turfing a number of people off their ancestral land in the process. Macdonald created a provincial tartan and put the image of the heroic, proud resistors to British rule at the heart of provincial identity.

As we saw in *Cornwallis: The Violent Birth of Halifax*, Edward Cornwallis founded modern Nova Scotia three years after he helped finish Bonnie Prince Charlie's Highland Army rebellion. Cornwallis led 320 soldiers through the Scottish Highlands in 1746, helping to destroy the ancient way of life.

A mere 190 years later, Macdonald turned his Nova Scotia into a gift shop for that ancient way of life.

★ ★ ★

As Cornwallis finally died in Gibraltar in 1776, British troops fought to destroy the Maroons in Jamaica.

The Maroons came from the Akan and Ashanti of Africa, brought into the British Empire as slaves and now living with hard-won freedom on the Caribbean island.

"Free-willed and spiritually independent, with strong kinship ties, they struggled and rebelled against slavery, and Spanish and British persecution, for more than 140 years," writes Dr. Henry Bishop, educator, consultant and former chief curator of the Black Cultural Centre for Nova Scotia.

The first thing anyone tells you about the Maroons is their ferocity, their pride, and their warrior spirit. Sitting like gods in the mountains of their adopted green, white, and gold Caribbean homeland, the Maroons arrived shortly after the Spanish in 1509. Spanish explorers mostly destroyed the indigenous Arawak through violence, slavery, and disease.

The Spanish outpost brought in captured men and women from Africa to replace them as enslaved workers. These Africans worked as cowboys, hunters, and herders, roaming the island with a freedom they'd never surrender.

And then England accidentally conquered Jamaica. In 1655, England tried to capture the wealth of Hispaniola (home to today's Dominican Republic and Haiti). It failed, but did take Jamaica from the Spanish – and that marked England's first colonial conquest.

As England struggled to gain control of the island, many Africans grabbed their freedom and took it to the hills.

They governed themselves and made it clear they sought no rulers. In their African homeland, their kin the Ashanti and Dahomey rose to imperial heights; these Jamaican freedom fighters possessed similar ambitions in Jamaica. We call them the Maroons, a word that once meant lost in the wilds.

* * *

The choice was stark. If you lived in the hills with the Maroons, you lived freely with your family. If you lived with the British in the lowlands, you lived under the slave-driver's whip.

From 1690 to 1820, 800,000 humans were shipped in chains to Jamaica, yet the population sank to 340,000. The Africans rose up to overthrow their English jailers, but England squashed revolts by burning and hanging the rebels. Rulers lashed rebels to wooden wagon wheels and beat them limb by limb, until their bodies broke. Uprisings in the 1600s and 1700s swelled the free Maroon ranks.

In 1690, a Maroon man called Cudjoe led attacks against England in the first Maroon War. For eighty-four years, three generations of Maroons assaulted the British slave-holders. The English government of Jamaica signed a peace treaty with the Maroons in 1739, ending that war. The peace acknowledged the freedom and independence of the Maroons, effectively creating two countries in Jamaica. The Maroons agreed to become slave-catchers, sending escaped black men and women back into the English chains.

Cudjoe's descendants moved to Trelawny Town in northwest Jamaica. Montague James became one of the elite war leaders for the people. His reputation grew in the 1770s and '80s, first in the service of the British as a captain, then as a free Maroon commander. The fifty-seven years of peace ended in 1795 when two Trelawny Maroons stole English pigs. They got caught. The Maroons were whipped by a runaway slave they had previously recaptured and returned to the English. The humiliation turned into rage and the Maroons expelled the English from Trelawny.

The second Maroon Wars erupted.

Jamaica's white minority, outnumbered ten to one, looked up to the mountains, dreading the descending apocalypse.

The Trelawny Maroons burned their own homes to the ground and climbed to the higher hills. Their three hundred isolated warriors faced 1,500 British troops supplied by a global empire. The Trelawny Maroons held two advantages: deep knowledge of the land and superb leadership.

In March 1796, the war suddenly stopped. The Maroons accepted an oppressive peace in exchange for the right to stay in Jamaica. But the promises vanished: the colonial authorities told the Trelawny Town

Maroons they faced deportation. The trapped warrior people moved to Montego Bay, then Kingston. The English offered some Maroons individual freedom, but most chose collective deportation. They chose family over freedom.

On June 4, 1796, the defeated Maroons boarded British military ships heading for Nova Scotia.

* * *

The 1700s were the century of displacement. The Maroons were banished to Nova Scotia. Only forty years earlier, the Acadians had been expelled from Nova Scotia. Loyalists, black and white, fled the American Revolution for Nova Scotia. And throughout it all, the Mi'kmaq fought a guerilla war against the British over their homeland Mi'kma'ki (also called Nova Scotia).

Sir John Wentworth, the lieutenant-governor of Nova Scotia, learned 568 angry Maroons were sailing his way. He also learned it was a felony to turn them back to Jamaica. He waited for HMS *Africa*, *Scorpion*, *Reasonable*, and *Iphigenia*. On board were 401 women, children, and old men, and 167 Maroon soldiers.

The *Iphigenia*, incidentally, was named for the Greek legend of a royal woman whose name means "she who causes the birth of strong offspring."

The British Crown put £25,000 behind the venture, hoping the free Maroons would accept domestication in Nova Scotia. Six weeks in transit showed promise; the rebels were reported to be quiet and well behaved. Only seventeen died en route. But the survivors cut military uniforms out of the linen scraps on the ship.

On July 21 and 22, the fog parted and three ships sailed into Halifax. Dozens of small craft swam at the foot of the big ships. Prince Edward Augustus, soon to be the commander-in-chief of British North America, welcomed the Maroons to Halifax. Edward Augustus found their "demeanour is lofty, their walk firm, and their persons erect. [They are] a smartly dressed body of men."

They were not to stay in Halifax, but to be settled, as least temporarily, outside of the new city. The hundreds of newcomers stayed at first on those ships, bobbing in the harbour, taking a good look at Halifax, while Halifax took a good look at them. Any fear the settlers had for the Maroons paled next to their fear of France. Halifax was forty-seven years old and its original fortifications had decayed. The Maroons were told to refortify the town, starting with Citadel Hill.

Edward Augustus, son of King George III, spent £100,000 a year to turn Halifax's scattered points of resistance into a cohesive fortification. Already, he had built his Martello towers and fortified George's Island, but he lost a crucial source of labour when Boston King and many other black Nova Scotians made the exodus to Sierra Leone four years earlier in 1792.

"The Maroons were landed a few days after their arrival and disposed of in as comfortable a manner as could be done at the very short notice we had of their arrival," Edward Augustus wrote. "Since which, at their own free will and option, a part of them have been daily employed in the new works on Citadel Hill, and in the same pay as His Majesty's troops."

It benefited both sides: the Maroons found good pay and useful work, while the local government re-fortified the city. Amazingly, the British seemed to have taken a people bent on destroying British fortifications in one place – Jamaica – and landed them as people bent on building British fortifications in another place – Nova Scotia. The ramshackle, expanding empire could be flexible when it needed to.

Most of the Maroons lived about two miles from the town so that they could easily walk to work each day. Oral history suggests this community sat where Africville would soon blossom, planting an important seed in the fledgling history of free black people in Halifax.

Wentworth wanted the Maroons to stay and assimilate. He hired Maroons to work at Government House. He did so "to remove all kinds of prepossessions against them from the minds of the inhabitants, and at the same time give encouragement and comfort to the Maroons," he wrote.

A tricky balance in a land where other black people could be bought and sold.

* * *

Wentworth gave his Bedford Basin home to Edward Augustus and set up a farm outside of Dartmouth. His house sat among rolling woods, lakes, and streams. Wentworth brought fifty Maroons with him to work the land. He called the land Preston (the same town Galloping Richard would later embrace as his own).

The Maroons weren't the first Africans to work the lands. Black Loyalists, fleeing American rebels for British promises, had briefly settled in the Preston area before migrating to Freetown.

Wentworth spoke highly of the Maroons. He wrote they were "perfectly quiet, orderly and peaceable." Everyone wondered how an African-Caribbean people would fare in a Nova Scotian winter. A friend warned Wentworth his relocation scheme amounted to "national murder." It would have been more humane to have killed them all in Jamaica than force them to freeze to death in Preston, the friend warned.

The Maroons crammed into a few winterized houses on the Wentworth estate and braced for the cold. Wentworth let slip that "a few men among them only appear to be ill tempered and dissatisfied."

Wentworth's plan to create a new village of Maroons outside of Halifax frightened some. His colleague from Jamaica, Commissary General William Dawes Quarrell, became sidelined by a "gouty bilious complaint," but from his bed predicted such a settlement wouldn't work. He wanted to scatter the Maroons among white settlements to diffuse the danger. The Maroons, having just picked family over freedom, seem unlikely to have welcomed this approach.

Henry Alline, an evangelist with the New Light Movement we saw earlier, described Halifax as "almost as dark and vile as Sodom." Few people – especially few black people – found it a friendly place to live.

* * *

In France, the new rebel government bloodily restructured society along the principles of liberty, equality, and fraternity, so the British king invaded. In Halifax, that meant guys out for a walk could be grabbed off the streets and forced to join the British military. It was called being press-ganged.

The Maroons valued Halifax little, but Halifax valued the Maroons as men ready to fight if France attacked the city. Maroon Captain Andrew Smith certainly thought they would. "They talk of the French coming here. If they do we are to be employed against them and by Heaven, cold as the weather may be, we will warm them every step of the road they take to Halifax," he wrote in a 1797 letter.

The Maroon soldiers worked well with Edward Augustus. "We are all anxious for an opportunity of shewing him that we are and ever will be a brave and loyal people and will die in defence of him, our King, or his good family," Smith concluded.

As John Grant notes in *The Maroons in Nova Scotia*, any Maroon person accused of an offence would be tried openly, and in the presence of at least three Maroon captains. Wentworth ordered handsome military uniforms for the Maroons and stocked their larders with seed and food.

* * *

You get a sense of sadness when you read about the Maroons' sojourn in Nova Scotia. One person wrote that the Maroons were "attached to gloomy superstitions of Africa." Wentworth tried to convert them into Church of England Christians. He sent them a chaplain who would teach the faith, and how to read and write. The Maroons opened a joint chapel-school in Preston in the fall of 1796.

Winter hit hard. A long, brutal affair, it tested the will of all Nova Scotians. Maroon people, accustomed to Jamaica's steady warmth, were ill-prepared for one of the worst winters to hit the colony. Many lost toes, feet, fingers, and hands.

The Maroons still attended school and church, but withdrew during times of disagreement with the British. Despite their openness to Anglican values, the Maroons still practised their traditional polygamy and buried their dead in the old way. When Christians moralized to them about the virtues of monogamy, many a Maroon retorted: "If we must abandon one or another of our wives, and children, which should it be?" The Maroon men mocked the British, vowing to take only one wife, so long as their other wives didn't object.

As for burial, the Christian rules bounced off Maroon culture. In Preston, English settlers observed them uncomfortably. When a person died, she was taken to a place of rest and covered under a mound of stones with items needed in the life to come, such as pipes, rum, and food. They sang ancient African burial songs, set to powerful drumming designed to draw ancestral spirits to the rites. Some speculated that the journey was back to Africa, in spiritual form. Many of the rituals bore strong resemblance to the practices of their Akan cousins in Ghana. The living and dead spoke through dance, music, and song, and prayers went to the divine via a spiritually gifted obeah.

The Maroons also valued hidden beliefs, known only to the initiated, so we are left guessing as to the true content of their ceremonies and souls. Many British seemed to genuinely believe it was their godly duty to convert the Maroons to a Church of England morality and went so far as to pay people to attend church.

The Maroons politely listened, and then ignored the surrounding European culture. More and more Maroons wondered why they should stay in Preston. Why should they curse their children to a life in this winter-wrecked land?

By the spring of 1797, many openly petitioned the British government to move them to a warmer part of the world. Some Maroons planned to conquer Guadalope, St. Domingo, Cuba, or Hispaniola, and build a new settlement for themselves in the Caribbean.

"Just put arms in our hands and land us anywhere in a warm climate, and we will make settlements and room for ourselves," the Maroons declared.

As conditions deteriorated, Maroon men and women refused to work, called in sick, or worked slowly in protest.

Wentworth asked them to work hard for one year; if still they wanted to leave, he would make arrangements. At the same time, Jamaica's government said it intended to stop funding the venture after 1798, reminding the Nova Scotia government that they were sent as "atrocious delinquents," not settlers.

Others raised fears that if they cut off assistance, the Maroons would pillage white settlements – just as they'd done in Jamaica. Wentworth wrote about the "aversions and abhorrence" European settlers felt toward the Maroons. "The Lieutenant-Governor could not have justified himself to His Majesty for permitting a people so lately in arms against his government and authority, and still complaining of injustice and ill treatment, to be located at a distance from the garrison of Halifax."

Fear burned in white hearts. Desire for a better life burned in black hearts.

★ ★ ★

A second long winter froze the Maroon resolve to leave. The six hundred people in Preston fractured into three groups under three leaders. Some turned against the original leadership that led them into Nova Scotia.

Maroon Captain Smith wrote to his brother Charles Samuels, who lived in England, that Nova Scotia made it hard to maintain a family as big as his. "You know I have four wives and eight small children besides our father, old Toe Williams, and our mother, sister," he wrote. Making it worse was "how strong parties run against me and the rest of our family for being the cause of bringing in the Maroons and surrendering their arms in the treaty."

Some called Smith a traitor and longed to be fighting back in Trelawny. Others questioned the effectiveness of the work strike. James William Dunbar, a Maroon, cut wood and fencing poles for the winter to help some friends. People who wanted the Maroons out of Nova Scotia punished him for making life here easier.

Another family planted potatoes and was punished. Fearing further retribution, the farmers fled the Preston settlement.

A pro-Nova Scotian group drifted away from the main body of Maroons. Led by James Palmer, the twenty-eight people settled in a place named Boydville. (Today, that area of Middle Sackville is called Maroon Hill.)

Palmer was a serious person. In Jamaica, he'd fought the British to the end and "breathed war and defiance." British authorities had offered a £100 bounty for his capture, dead or alive. But now he wanted peace. The group he led had mostly converted to Christianity and enthusiastically cultivated the new land. They soon sold surplus berries, eggs, poultry, pigs, brooms, and baskets to the Halifax market. The group attracted more members and by 1799, sixty people called Maroon Hill home.

That same year, Maroon leaders in Preston began extended negotiations to follow the Black Loyalists who migrated to Sierra Leone. In March 1799, the Sierra Leone Company agreed to settle the Maroons in the African colony. The company insisted the Maroons be settled far away from the "Nova Scotians," the Black Loyalists, to prevent trouble in the form of the two peoples uniting and working together. Work stopped in Preston and Maroon Hill. The government withheld supplies.

The ship that was to take them to Africa failed to arrive, forcing another winter in 1800. The "insistence on speed had merely led to more antagonism between whites and blacks in Nova Scotia, since all had expected to be rid of the problem long before Christmas," wrote one observer.

Some worked on in Halifax, building Government House.

* * *

Finally, in the summer of 1800, the *Asia* arrived in Halifax. On August 3, 550 people boarded the ship (151 men, 177 women, and 222 children). Not all of the Maroons left; pockets of individuals and families decided Nova Scotia offered better futures and so stayed on.

Wentworth insisted everybody be sent to Africa and searched the territory to force reluctant Maroons to leave. He didn't get them all. On August 7 or 8, the Maroons left Halifax harbour for the long journey returning them to the land of their ancestors.

In a strange twist, Robin W. Winks, author of *The Blacks in Canada: A History*, reports that the Maroons offered to take five hundred slaves from West Africa and send them to Nova Scotia to replace the Maroon labour pool.

The offer was apparently declined.

On September 30, the *Asia* made land and the Maroons stepped out into Freetown. Liberia boiled in open rebellion. Some Black Loyalists went to war with the Sierra Leone Company for control of the land. Historian James Walker records the African Nova Scotians drew up a settler constitution that "was a declaration of Nova Scotian independence from the company government."

The Maroons joined the government forces and helped crush the Nova Scotian uprising.

* * *

John Grant, in *The Maroons in Nova Scotia*, gets to the core reason the Maroons are so well remembered by so many Nova Scotians centuries later. "Like the Highlanders of Scotland, the real spiritual ancestors of many white Nova Scotians whose collective memory is stirred by the vision of kilted warriors pouring out of their hills, their banners flying, their pipes bawling, and their claymores flashing in the sun, to avenge some real or imagined insult, or to rally for some lost cause, the Maroons represent the indomitable pride of being to many black Nova Scotians," he writes. "The Maroons, like the Scottish Highlanders, possessed characteristics that we might not always want our children to emulate, but in time of need they are the spiritual ancestors who recall group pride, the inner sense of dignity, the cohesion and the strength that can provide a people with the will to carry on."

The Maroons are a crucial clue to solving the riddle of *Redemption Songs*. They tie Nova Scotia to Jamaica. They bring black pride to Nova Scotia. Let's jump ahead a century to rejoin Marcus Garvey – the man who would turn that pride into a global movement.

Song 10: An Orgy of Violence

Dave Eshelman chose the summer fake-prison job at Stanford University over work at a pizza joint and quickly became the most sadistic of the guards. Forty years after the project, he reflected that he took to the brutal role so quickly because he didn't know any of the prisoners – he feared anyone who knew him would have seen right through the act.

"What came over me was not an accident. It was planned," he said in 2011. He acted like a thug guard and waited for someone to stop him, but no one did. At what point does a fake personality become your real identity?

Eshelman said he could easily imagine himself as one of the American soldiers tormenting Iraqi prisoners in Iraq's notorious Abu Grahib jail. "Sometimes when people know about the experiment and then meet me, it's like, My God this guy's a psycho! But everyone who knows me would just laugh," he said.

Richard Yacco played one of Eshelman's prisoners. Decades later, he seemed undamaged by the event, but deeply reflective. He was astonished at how easily he fell into the role of prisoner, and how readily he accepted the fate society laid out for him. He wondered what implications it held for the young men and women he taught at a public high school in Oakland, California.

"If you believe society has assigned you a role, do you then assume the characteristics of that role?" he asked in 2011.

Yacco's students were poor. Going to high school created better opportunities for the young men and women, but few opportunities translated into success. He concluded that students learned at a young age that they were "prisoners" and so most of them naturally assumed that was true and prepared for that destiny.

★ ★ ★

Marcus Garvey utterly rejected the future his society planned for him and created his own destiny.

After prophesying that a black king would rise in Africa, Garvey landed in Harlem as the renaissance bloomed in the spring of 1916.

People who'd never left New York jostled with new arrivals from the southern states as they passed migrants from the West Indies. Lovers' murmurs whispered under shouted orders, muted by screaming arguments, noted by street preachers and politicians. The air teased the nose with the fragrances of home cooking and street eating. Kids ran lottery numbers to kingpins as zoot-suited men walked arm-linked with

Josephine Baker-inspired women. Old ladies born into slavery passed middle-aged men delighted to no longer have to scrape before every southern white boy, observed by West Indies youth alien to the deference culture.

Garvey soon saw that black comes in many colours.

The ebullient jubilance of southern Baptists clashed against the quiet reserve of many West Indies people. While those escaping southern poverty took any work offered, most West Indies migrants arrived to ply their skilled trades. Wilfred Domingo, a colleague of Garvey's from Jamaica, wrote that people from the Caribbean sought "positions that the average African-American has been schooled to regard as restricted to white men."

They didn't know they were supposed to be prisoners.

At twenty-nine, Garvey started over again, and not for the last time. In just a few years, those tens of thousands of strangers would line the streets to catch a glimpse of the same man parading through Harlem as the President of Africa.

But first he had to find the words to win the masses. He secured lodgings in a small, stuffy bedroom perched above the vibrant streets. He lived on tinned sardines, corned beef hash, beans, and canned soup. His asthma flared up, making it hard to find enough air to work. He finally found a job plying his old trade of printing.

★ ★ ★

Garvey planned to raise money through public speaking to fund UNIA causes in Jamaica. But nobody would pay to see Marcus Garvey speak back then, so he sought a star co-speaker.

Garvey, as always, aimed for the top. He walked into the NAACP offices and asked W.E.B. Du Bois, the most famous black man in America, to speak at the event. Du Bois was away, so Garvey left a note with his request. He also registered the many white people running the National Association for the Advancement of Colored People.

Du Bois did not agree to speak, and he didn't attend Garvey's talk. Hardly anybody did. Garvey fell off the stage mid-speech. He blamed nerves and exhaustion.

His unbreakable spirit instructed him to ignore the empty house in Harlem and set out on a nationwide tour. He expressed confidence his people were out there – and he would go find them. The restless wanderer moved again, this time south, to learn of the black situation there first-hand among the ten million men, women, and children who remained south of the Mason-Dixon line.

The south shocked him. Up north, he sat wherever he wanted on the trains, but down south, his African DNA meant he was forced to ride on shoddy trains, barred him from drinking at certain water fountains, and generally told he was less of a man than someone with European DNA.

Garvey could no longer eat in the dining car, nor sleep in the sleeping area. Outside the windows, the KKK recruited new members, burned crosses, and murdered humans due to the colour of their skin.

Mobs mutilated the genitals of black men, burned them alive, hanged them, and then hacked their bodies into pieces of meat – souvenirs to carry home

In six months, Garvey travelled across thirty-eight states. He listened to preachers and congregations, studying their songs and prayers. Many lived in constant fear of white terrorism as they tried to lift their families out of the poverty left by slavery.

Garvey ended his pilgrimage in Atlanta. He set up another public talk, introducing himself as Professor Garvey, "an orator of exceptional force [who] has spoken to packed audiences in New York, Washington, Philadelphia, Louisville, Nashville." He laid out a vision of black-run banks, theatres, and other industries, arguing that economic freedom created most other types of freedom.

He returned to Harlem in 1917. He invited Theodore Roosevelt, the former U.S. president, to his homecoming talk. Roosevelt did not attend. Garvey told a small crowd about his trip. But if you only watched him, you'd think he spoke to millions.

Garvey now had the ideas that would create Garveyism.

★ ★ ★

Every time Garvey stepped out of his cramped apartment, he walked into the open-air university that was the Harlem Renaissance. Street preachers climbed stepladders and addressed impromptu crowds numbering in the hundreds.

The stepladder preachers cared little for the established elite and earned their crowds through charisma and intellectual force. They didn't book halls and ask people to attend their talks; they went directly to the people and spoke to them in their streets. Many of these radicals were from the West Indies.

Garvey listened to a popular socialist speaker named A. Philip Randolph. When Randolph stepped down from his ladder, he offered the platform to Garvey. Garvey climbed up and boomed his words over Harlem. People started to listen to him. It turned out he didn't need to borrow star power to draw a crowd; he became the star.

The Black Moses tapped into people fed up with second-class lives. Garvey brought a new solution. He didn't want to improve conditions in America – he was coming to see that country as a lost cause.

Hubert Harrison, a famous orator known as the Black Socrates, spoke in Harlem in June 1917. His star power drew a crowd of two thousand, and he offered the audience to Garvey. "This was Harlem's first real sight of Garvey. His magnetic personality, torrential eloquence and intuitive knowledge of crowd psychology were all brought into play," wrote one man who saw his debut. "He swept the audience along with him." Garvey unlocked his secret power: not speaking his own mind, but speaking the minds of his people.

★ ★ ★

The Black Socrates soon called the Black Moses the greatest orator ever heard in the Negro world. Garvey's rise coincided with the rising question of how black leaders should think about the Great War in Europe.

W.E.B. Du Bois took a patriotic tone, urging his

people to fight with their fellow Americans on European battlefields. In 1916, an all-black regiment called the 369th stirred pride in many hearts. Some 500,000 African-Americans signed up in July 1917. Garvey initially backed the general pro-war mood, but began to shift his position. He was twenty-nine, but his asthma rendered him unfit to fight.

In 1916, a ship of Jamaican soldiers sailed for England. Enemy ships drove the *Verdala* off course and it sought refuge in Halifax. But it hit a spring blizzard off the Nova Scotia coast and the soldiers, dressed in uniforms designed for Jamaican warmth, suffered badly from frostbite; some died. Those who survived joined the millions and millions of men running into enemy machine guns, flame-throwers, and tanks as Europe turned into an open grave.

Du Bois saw the black war effort as a crucial fulcrum that could be used to lever full citizenship in America. Garvey disagreed and turned against the "white man's war." Black men and women in America and Canada died in appalling numbers, and died in segregation. Even in the dank, hellish trenches, society found room to lower the situation of black soldiers by forcing them to use inferior tools. "Why go over to Europe and fight for the whites and lose an arm or leg when you can fight for a just cause?" Garvey asked.

Many leaders put a higher value on ending lynchings and bringing democracy to black men and women in the United States, over defending freedom in Europe. No conscription without representation, Garvey and the other street preachers insisted

In East St. Louis, a group of white men attacked a black neighbourhood and set it on fire.

They gunned down people as they fled their burning homes. Humans were strung up from telegraph poles. Any black person who tried to escape East St. Louis faced a firing line akin to a German trench. White women beat black women half to death. One group of white men grabbed a black man, put a rope around his neck, and ripped his scalp off his head so he bled into his face as he died. The fighting lasted through May and July 1917.

Garvey began talking about armed self-defence. He spoke in New York, detailing the massacre in what his biographer Colin Grant, in *Negro with a Hat: The Rise and Fall of Marcus Garvey*, called "a prolonged howl of outrage." He argued that southern power-brokers leaned on northern politicians to permit such violence to deter African-Americans from leaving the south. Southerners wanted to keep their "labour serfs," he argued, and so the north held a Roman holiday where "the mob feasted on the blood of the Negro."

"This is no time for fine words, but a time to lift one's voice against the savagery of a people who claim to be the dispensers of democracy," he cried over a loud drum of applause, cheers, and groans. "The black man has always trusted the white man. He has always clung to him as a brother man. When there was no white man in Africa to help the sickly and dying Livingstone, the black man, ever true, even as Simon of Cyrenia was true in bearing the cross of the despised Jesus, came to the rescue," he said. "The Negro in American history … has demonstrated to the American Nation that he is as true as steel. Yet for all his services he receives the reward of lynching, burning and wholesale slaughter."

Garvey printed his speech and spread it far and wide, building his following. He sent money to rebuild the broken community in East St. Louis. He hoped he could be the bond that united the African diaspora. "White people are taking advantage of black men today because black men all over the world are disunited," he said.

Black people learned to watch white people closely. It was clear trouble was brewing when white groups with picnic baskets and snacks appeared – a sure sign that a lynching was coming.

Garvey added one important person to his audience: J. Edgar Hoover, head of the FBI. Hoover spied on Garvey and wrote down his speeches.

A UNIA pamphlet quoted a new recruit saying, "Garvey gave my people backbones where they had wishbones."

★ ★ ★

Garvey's people in Cape Breton heard him, and straightened their backbones. Garvey was not the only West Indies person to leave the islands to escape poverty. In the early 1900s, the Dominion Iron and Steel Company opened a new plant in Sydney, Nova Scotia, and recruited workers from around the world. Hundreds of men and their families left Grenada, St. Vincent, and British Guyana to move to Cape Breton, giving the island its first big black presence. Most settled in the community of Whitney Pier. They joined a small number of African-Nova Scotians descended from the Black Loyalists.

The men came to work the coal mines and steel plants, but were trained as tailors, carpenters, coppersmiths, tinsmiths, bricklayers, farmers, barbers, fishermen, and horsemen. Most spoke English and many belonged to the Anglican Church, making life in the British-rooted Cape Breton accessible. A photo of the local 1901 coronation parade for King Edward VII shows several black men attending to a float in Sydney, proving the black community was planted there very early in the century.

The men worked in the blast furnaces and coke ovens, alongside other immigrants and poor local whites. The men toiled in the dirtiest, most dangerous parts of the operation, and for little money. White men tended to work the slightly more comfortable hearth. Many of the immigrants soon left the mines to start their own businesses. Soon black-run taverns, stores, and restaurants opened.

Dominion Coal liked to keep ethnic groups together, so it employed people of the same race in the same mines and housed them together. Cape Breton's new black community was joined by an Italian community and a Belgium Town.

In 1918, Albert Francis decided Cape Breton's West Indies immigrants needed a central place to gather. He had arrived from Barbados in 1916 – the year Garvey issued his prophecy – and worked the No. 16 Colliery in New Waterford. He gathered several West Indians in his backyard one day and pitched them on listening to Garvey and building a Universal Negro Improvement Association hall.

The association got its first charter in 1920 and spent a decade raising money to build the hall. The men and women who belonged to the UNIA barely earned enough to feed and shelter their families, but they put money aside for the greater good. In 1932, they celebrated the opening of the first UNIA hall in Nova Scotia, which was probably the first UNIA hall in all of Canada.

Alongside the New Waterford UNIA came associations in Glace Bay and Sydney. They read the words of Marcus Garvey and opened community halls there, too. They also started the Coloured Athletic and Dramatic Club and the Ever-Ready Club. Not everything was political.

★ ★ ★

Marcus Garvey began to see a patriotic trap. Black North Americans had fought for democracy abroad, but now they had to fight for it at home, too. Some white North Americans rested complacently on the belief that North America was the Promised Land and believed black people had it so good they'd never leave. Why bother changing things for people with so little power and so few options?

Garvey believed he saw a way out: bring the diaspora back to Africa in an idea called African Redemption.

In August 1918, the thirty-one-year-old launched *Negro World*, yet another journal recording his thoughts and the thoughts of other prominent leaders. Many began calling the UNIA the Garvey Movement, and his ideas Garveyism. He spurned advertising, believing it weakened the paper's message, and gave copies away. He despised hair-straightening products and skin-lightening cosmetics, instead founding his pride in his dark skin. He said skin bleaches libelled the race. The desire to look white acted as a visible chain of mental slavery, he argued. "Take the kinks out of your mind, instead of out of your hair," he said.

In Harlem, the UNIA became as a business incubator, opening restaurants, ice-cream parlours, and tea rooms. Garvey laid the groundwork for the Black Star Line, a planned black-run shipping company to rival White Star, the company behind famous ships including *Titanic*. His journal rejoiced in the success of African-American businesses and encouraged more. Money invested in such companies doubled as investments in the black race itself, he said.

J. Edgar Hoover tried to sweep him up in a Red Scare deportation, but could not build a case to expel the Jamaican.

"The time for cowardice is past. The old-time Negro has gone – buried with Uncle Tom," Garvey stated.

★ ★ ★

On September 2, 1918, Cape Breton's West Indies immigrants held the annual Colored Picnic on South Street in Glace Bay. They organized a bicycle race, which evidently was open to all. An Italian man identified only as L. Linello pulled into the lead, but came off his bike. A newspaper reporter blamed an unidentified black man, claiming he'd pushed the speedy Italian to the ground. Other people said the cyclist ran straight into the black man, who got knocked over and blamed for the accident.

Whatever really happened, the Italian attacked the black man, and soon other Italians and other black men rushed in to try and even the fight. "Soon, a free-for-all fight was in progress," the reporter wrote.

The scuffle escalated into a brawl, which spiralled into a race riot. Officials called soldiers and police officers to stop the violence. They failed The September 3 edition of the Sydney *Record* blasted this headline: MURDER DONE IN WILD RIOT OF NEGROES AND WHITES IN GLACE BAY.

The subhead put one version of events to ink: ATTACK ON ITALIAN BICYCLE RIDER AT NEGROES' PICNIC PRECIPITATED HOURS OF WILD EXCITEMENT AND ORGY OF VIOLENCE.

Whites armed themselves and rushed to the riot. Blacks gathered in their homes. From three p.m. until ten p.m., the rioting burned on. White men tore through the picnic grounds, destroying the refreshment booths and everything else. Black families fled. The white men raced after them, caught some, and beat them viciously. Other white people opened their doors to the fleeing families, but they soon had their own windows smashed and doors broken by mobs. "The refugees were dragged out in the street and battered and hammered in wild anger," the newspaper records.

The mayor literally read the riot act and the soldiers broke up the fighting, "but not before scores of negroes had been beaten and kicked by the infuriated whites, some of them into insensibility." Guns, clubs, and rocks were deployed as weapons. Police, backed by the army, sought to end the riot by arresting "every black man in sight."

Frustrated, the white mob walked into a black settlement in an area called the Stirling and shot off revolvers. The black people in the houses shot back. A man named Irvin Yard (also known as Hernan or

Urban Yard), standing upstairs in one house, took a bullet to the heart – a bullet fired, the newspaper said, "presumably by one of his own race." Everyone in his house was taken to jail for questioning or protection.

Black men returning home from work found agitated white mobs chasing them. One man fled to the end of the Quarry Point road and leapt off the wharf to escape the attackers. The mob "fished him out and beat him." Another black man sprinted for a half a mile before collapsing. The mob mauled him.

Besides Yard's murder, several white and black men were badly hurt. Two white men – Joe Hart and Billy MacLean – went to hospital with bullets in them, but survived. Another black man lost his nose and parts of his face in a razor attack. "And 33 coloured men are in jail for protection or arrest, many of them with injuries which may disable them for life," the article reported. By midnight, a large crowd gathered outside the police station and wanted to have at the black people inside. But the white police force held their nerve and kept their prisoners safe.

"The affair has created a tremendous sensation and feeling is still tense here," the newspaper continued. "For some of the time past, the feeling of white against black has been growing bitter and on several occasions serious fights ensued. It is now imperative that the colored settlement be moved beyond the limits of the town and that no further permits be granted for the holding of such demonstrations, as the negroes' Monday picnic … until adequate police protection can be provided."

The coroner investigated Yard's killing, but gathered no evidence to shed light on who pulled the trigger. Coroner Ogilvie heard from five black witnesses that a white man had shot Yard in the heart as Yard stood in his window looking out at the mob. Other witnesses said two black men in another house had fired shots into the advancing mob. Police thought it likely that one of those shots had somehow deflected upward and killed Yard.

"It will probably never be found out who shot Yard," the Sydney *Record* concluded, accurately.

Calm minds prevailed the next day and the violence did not resume. The *Record* reporter toured the black neighbourhoods and found the mob had demolished several homes. Black men limped the streets bruised and bandaged.

On September 4, the *Sydney Daily Post* reported quiet in Glace Bay, too. The next day, the *Record* reported that while Yard's killer remained at large, police arrested "two burly negroes" blamed for starting the riot. The *Daily Post* described them as "big, powerful-looking men." The reporter thought little of their brains, noting "it has often been said that in the head is no place to hit a Negro if one wishes to place him out of action."

It also reported that several taxi drivers were in trouble for allegedly driving black men home to arm themselves and then driving them back to the riot. Soldiers and police stayed in the area to quell any further fighting.

"Most of the blacks have decided that discretion is the better part of valor, that distance lends enchantment, in fact, they have concluded that the Hub [area of Glace Bay] is a much safer place for them than at the Stirling," the *Record* reported.

The reporter said that by Saturday, he expected not a single coloured man would be living in the Stirling (also spelled Sterling). They moved to the Hub. "Had they done that long ago, as your correspondent has suggested more than once, the town would have been spared many riots."

The coroner's jury concluded the investigation into Yard's killing by saying a "person unknown" had shot him, and that was the end of the matter.

Gordon Sheriff was one of the three bicycle riders in contention to win the picnic race. He saw the race riot from the centre. But by 1961, he said merely that "two bikes touched and fell" and the two riders got into a fist fight as friends joined in. No mention of race. Sheriff, the newspaper noted, kept on pedalling and rode all the way home without stopping.

The 1961 newspaper reporter concluded by wryly noting that "of course, the winner of the race was never determined."

A murderous race riot had morphed into an amusing anecdote.

⋆ ⋆ ⋆

Garvey shocked his followers – and his enemies – by speaking proudly of Mother Africa, and of talking about a homecoming to the ancestral land. In a famous post-war speech called "If you believe the Negro has a soul," Garvey laid out his planned African Redemption.

"It is for me to inform you that the Universal Negro Improvement Association is an organization that seeks to unite, into one solid body, the four hundred million Negroes in the world," he began, "for the purpose of bettering our industrial, commercial, educational, social, and political conditions."

He continued in his hypnotizing, rapid-fire delivery.

"As you are aware, the world in which we live today is divided into separate race groups and distinct nationalities. Each race and each nationality is endeavoring to work out its own destiny, to the exclusion of other races and other nationalities. We hear the cry of 'England for the Englishman,' of 'France for the Frenchman,' of 'Germany for the German,' of 'Ireland for the Irish,' of 'Palestine for the Jew,' of 'Japan for the Japanese,' of 'China for the Chinese.'

"We of the Universal Negro Improvement Association are raising the cry of 'Africa for the Africans,' those at home and those abroad."

He turned the stain of "one drop" of black blood cursing a person into a great blessing. Lucky were those who could claim an honest slice of the great African heritage. He planned to overthrow four hundred years of slavery-induced separation and unite the children of the diaspora. He claimed the UNIA had "worked wonders" in this cause, largely through his endless travel across North, South, and Central America.

"It is for this purpose, that we are asking you to join our land and to do the best you can to help us to bring about an emancipated race," he said. "We want every Negro to work for one common object, that of building a nation of his own on the great continent of Africa." He looked at Africa and saw not humanity's past, but its future.

He planned to start a prosperous, industrial,

commercially successful nation. He believed it could happen in a matter of a few years. He pointed to UNIA footholds in Nigeria. He drew inspiration from the Jewish efforts to build a homeland in the Middle East, a land that would eventually become Israel.

"If you believe that the Negro has a soul, if you believe that the Negro is a man, if you believe the Negro was endowed with the senses commonly given to other men by the Creator, then you must acknowledge that what other men have done, Negroes can do," Garvey said, rising to his conclusion. "We want to build up cities, nations, governments, industries of our own in Africa, so that we will be able to have a chance to rise from the lowest to the highest position in the African Commonwealth."

The festering wound of slavery could finally grow over; it would have been a terrible exile, but the exodus would end. His Nova Scotian followers knew that back-to-Africa could really be done – many Black Loyalists and Maroons now lived in Sierra Leone.

In the aftermath of the Great War, the European powers grappled over colonial control in Africa. Ireland violently fought its British rulers in the Easter Rising. Russians tossed off the yoke of serfdom in a revolution. The UNIA planned to send a delegate to the 1919 Versailles Peace Conference as part of a wider International League for Darker People.

Garvey's moment had come.

★ ★ ★

Over eighteen months, the UNIA in Harlem swelled from thirteen members to 5,500 members. It opened branches in twenty-five states, along with the

Canadian offices, and ones in the West Indies, West Africa, and Central America. Garvey claimed two million followers; critics said it was more like 300,000 paying members.

Garvey sped through the streets of Harlem standing on the running board of a Cadillac, shouting through a megaphone, "Africa for the Africans!"

The Versailles mission failed. Du Bois, representing the NAACP, pushed the case to include black Africans in the peace. The European delegates ignored him, and they ignored Garvey, too. The two leaders drifted apart from each other as Du Bois focused on improving life in black America while Garvey looked to Africa.

The victorious European countries took control of German Africa. France and Britain partitioned Togoland and the Cameroons. Great Britain seized German East Africa, with Belgium pulling off a bone of that empire, too. White-run South Africa took Namibia.

Garvey called it the "Pieces Conference, because its unholy intent in depriving men of their liberty has made no headway for the restoration of peace." He shot back with the Black Star Line. The people who had arrived on slave ships would now run steamships.

★ ★ ★

"Garvey shouted words, words spinning like bullets, words falling like bombs, sharp words like poisoned daggers, thundering words and phrases lit with all the hues of the rainbow to match the wild, approving roar of his people," wrote Claude McKay, a Garveyite who often contributed to *Negro World*.

At a time when many businesses would not serve black people, Black Star formed the core of the UNIA's ambitious plans for black-run businesses, shops, and factories. Garvey reasoned that a person with enough money can buy just about anything – including his freedom. The children of the self-emancipated slaves who earned their liberty in Nova Scotia knew this to be true.

Black Star Line, borrowing the glorious robes of White Star Line's powerful brand, showed black people deserved the good life. Perhaps the idea first crept into Garvey's imagination as he switched from a good seat to a black seat as he trained across the Mason-Dixon line.

He dove into the oceanic project with little preparation or planning. "He turned the pages of his past life as an avid reader turns the pages of an adventure story," wrote his second wife, Amy Jacques. "Those who get hurt in these tense moments of the adventure are only regarded as necessary proper to the build-up of the hero. He was quite as impersonal in this regard as any reader."

He could turn viciously on anyone – especially any black person – who questioned his plans. He climbed back up his street stepladder and branded opponents as people who had lost their minds to the white propaganda that a black man could build nothing, but was only fit to work like a mule. Garvey descended the stepladder into a sea of cheering faces.

★ ★ ★

Hampton Smith was a brutal man who in 1918 ran a Georgia plantation like he still owned black people.

One time he went too far and severely beat a worker. Sidney Johnson, eighteen, had seen enough and killed Smith. Some local white people sought revenge. They couldn't find Johnson so, after a week, grabbed a different black man and murdered him. This man's name was Hayes Turner.

Turner had nothing to do with Smith's death, but he would die for it. His wife, Mary Turner, eight months' pregnant, tried to save him. Several hundred people chased her down, tied her upside down from a tree, doused her in gas and oil, and burned her alive. Men cut open her stomach, pulled out the baby, and killed him, too.

Garvey exploded in rage. "Since it is not safe to lynch a white man in any part of America, we shall press the button and lynch him in the great continent of Africa," he roared.

★ ★ ★

In October 1919, George Tyler walked through the front door of Garvey's office and shot him four times. The first bullet flew past, but the second sliced the skin on his head and the next two thumped into his legs. Garvey fell bleeding in shock while his wife and others wrestled the would-be assassin away. Tyler escaped but was arrested later that day. The next day, while in jail and in police custody, Tyler jumped through a third-floor window, apparently trying to escape, thereby falling to his death. Some had doubts it was a suicide or an escape attempt. The press suggested Tyler was motivated by UNIA's refusal to invest in a business he owned. There was further speculation that the shooting was ordered by Edwin Kilroe, a New York City assistant district attorney.

Five days later, Garvey rose from his hospital bed and travelled to Philadelphia for a planned speech. Garvey's resurrection stirred powerful emotions. The Black Moses seemed divinely sent to organize the exodus to Africa. He stood fearless before his people. "If the shots caused the organization to advance 2,000 per cent, then I am satisfied to die," he said.

As Garvey became Garveyism, his oration soared. He preached to a packed Madison Square Garden, where thousands of people stood waving the UNIA flag of red, green, and black. Red for the blood spilled; green for Africa; black for the chosen people.

He took the stage with the celebrated Captain Joshua Cockburn, the black man who would captain Black Star Line's first ship. "We Negroes are now whetting up the swords to fight for freedom and if the white people treat us right, we will combine; otherwise, the Negroes will join Japan and the East," he reportedly said, even as the last peace treaties of the First World War were yet to be written.

The next day, Garvey boarded the *Yarmouth*, which was to be Black Star's first ship. Thousands joined him in a moment of great excitement. A lucky few hundred who had bought passage joined him for the maiden voyage of the first black-run and black-owned shipping company in the world. Many had scorned Garvey and doubted his plan, saying it couldn't be done; the sound of the ship's horn echoed his rebuke over New York City.

His supporters had bought $600,000 worth of stock in the shipping line, usually at great personal sacrifice. Black Star Line incorporated on June 27, 1919, bought the *Yarmouth* that fall, and made the short maiden voyage on October 31.

"The Eternal has happened," Garvey later wrote in *Negro World*. "For centuries, the black man has been taught by his ancient overlords that he was 'nothing,' is 'nothing,' and shall never be 'anything.' Five years ago the Negro was sleeping upon his bale of cotton in the South of America; he was steeped in the mud in the banana fields of the West Indies and Central America, seeing no possible way of extricating himself from the environments; he smarted under the lash of the new taskmaster in Africa; but … today he is a new man."

In the October edition of *Negro World*, writer William Ferris put it this way: "What we need is another Emancipator who will tell the Negro youth, 'You can succeed in big business just as you succeed along the other lines of intellectual and mechanical endeavour. You can even sail the high seas and run a steamship line.'"

Garvey's soul-lifting poetry raced around the world, wooing ears all the way up to Nova Scotia.

★ ★ ★

Garvey built an Africa of the imagination. It stood in sharp contrast to the usual depiction of Africa as a land of savage nightmares. It seemed like no one could actually depict real life in Africa.

But Garvey could add the African Legion, uniformed, armed men who attended parades for the

UNIA. While many snickered at his apparent fantasy life, a lot of people admired him for not begging for white approval, but defining his own success.

"The Negro who slept and wallowed in the mire for centuries has just begun to turn and he now has placed his hope in God and himself and he is going forward to achieve," Garvey said.

The *Yarmouth*, nearly flooded by financial and mechanical troubles, made its first real trip in late 1919, sailing for Cuba. One can imagine the extraordinary experience of an ordinary black woman, long conditioned to see her skin as the determining, failing characteristic of her humanity, and never thinking to question that white skin ruled the world, stepping on board a ship filled with black passengers, crewed by black sailors, and run by black business people.

Most people started calling the ship the *Frederick Douglass*, though it legally remained the *Yarmouth*.

Garvey's arrival on board the *Yarmouth* brought thousands out in Havana, including the Cuban president, who held a banquet in his honour.

Garvey, with a full head of steam, married Amy Ashwood that same year. The couple honeymooned in Canada, visiting Toronto and Montreal in what was likely the first trip to the country for both of them.

* * *

He returned to an America that had decided to make alcohol illegal. This was not a personal problem, as Garvey did not drink, but it was a professional problem. The Black Star Line operated a lucrative trade in liquor.

The UNIA held its First International Convention in 1920 and elected Garvey the provisional President of Africa. The convention's theme was, "How much will you give to help redeem Africa and thereby your own race?"

Garvey had made clear he would give everything he had, and would inspire the same from his followers. "In the full glare of the limelight, the Marcus Garvey I knew receded into the shadows. The public figure Garvey took his place," his wife later wrote.

Under the pressure, the marriage buckled and broke. Marcus Garvey and Amy Ashwood divorced in 1922 after three years of marriage.

★ ★ ★

The Black Moses let his personal life be drowned in the Red Sea and stepped forth to set his people free. The massive gathering in New York brought Garveyism into the mainstream.

At two p.m. on August 1, 1922, a grand parade left the UNIA offices and headed through Harlem led by four mounted police. Garvey, ennobled in robes, his majestic head crowned with a plumed, bicornate helmet, sat in an open car, his stern face gazing levelly at the spectators. Seated beside him was Gabriel Johnson, mayor of Monrovia, Liberia. The brass band marched ahead, leading Black Cross nurses in pristine uniforms; the crew of the *Yarmouth*; more than five hundred automobiles; and UNIA marchers, who bore incendiary banners: Down with Lynching; [Haitian revolutionary] Toussaint L'Ouverture was an abler soldier than Napoleon; Garvey, the Man of the Day.

His day had indeed come. As President of Africa, he saw himself as the leader of 400 million scattered people, a government in fractured exile. His planned country would be the third free African country – only Liberia and Ethiopia escaped colonial rule. The bands played "Onward Christian Soldiers" as the regal procession entered Madison Square Garden – packed with 25,000 humans.

On the anniversary of emancipation day in the Caribbean, Marcus Mosiah Garvey spoke to his people.

"For over three hundred years we who are denizens of this Western Hemisphere have been held in slavery. For that period of time we have been separated from our brothers and sisters in the great continent of Africa, but this Sunday morning brings Negroes from every country together," he preached.

Garvey brought kind wishes from prominent Zionists, who saw a kindred spirit trying to reclaim ancestral land. If Jewish people wished to return to Israel, why shouldn't Africans desire a return to Africa?

Garvey shared a letter he had written to the great Irish leader Eamon de Valera, wedding the dream of a free Ireland to the dream of a free Africa.

"We are assembled here tonight as the descendants of a suffering people and we are determined to suffer no longer! Wheresoever I go, whether it is England, France or Germany, I am told, This is the white man's country. Wheresoever I travel throughout the United States of America, I am made to understand that I am a 'n'," he said, declining to utter the hateful word.

"If the Englishman claims England as his native habitat, and the Frenchman claims France, the time has come for the 400 million Negroes to claim Africa as their native land," Garvey cried over a rising tide of cheers. "If you believe that the Negro should be one vast empire, controlled by the Negro, then rise."

They did, singing the UNIA anthem: "Ethiopia, Thou Land of Our Fathers."

Ethiopia, thou land of our fathers,
Thou land where the gods loved to be
As storm cloud at night suddenly gathers
Our armies come rushing to see

And the chorus:

Advance, advance to victory
Let Africa be free;
Advance to meet the foe
With the might
Of the red, the black and the green

The conference made news around the globe, bringing Garveyism to millions of people. It inspired unrest in Belgian Congo, where *Negro World* sparked a liberty movement.

What he represented was not simply emancipation – individual freedom – but the idea of emancipation, the possibility of freedom. He was bold, brave, beautiful, capable of assembling massive crowds, of starting shipping lines, of dreaming of Africa – of making Africa a place one could honourably dream about. He drew his confidence and self-respect from black people – not from whites.

People noticed.

★ ★ ★

The British newspaper *The Daily Telegraph* mocked Garvey's ambition of an independent Africa. "History has never been able to find a time when the Negroid races were the real masters of Africa, unless it was in the Paleolithic age," it concluded. The reporter believed that without European rule, African countries would collapse and all humans would return to the wild.

Other newspapers calmly identified black people as the missing link between human and ape. "A few days ago [they] told us that [boxer] Jack Johnson, being a Negro, was only a few degrees removed from the gorilla," Garvey replied. "But apes never wrote books. Apes never wrote a bill of rights."

And Garvey's convention did indeed write a bill of rights, with fifty-four resolutions designed to improve the condition of the African diaspora.

"We strongly condemn the cupidity of those nations of the world who, by open aggression or secret schemes, have seized the territories and inexhaustible natural wealth of Africa, and we place on record our most solemn determination to reclaim the treasures and possessions of the vast continent of our forefathers," it said.

Garvey trod the stage of the great convention dressed in red robes and a gold-tasselled turban. He was the first black president of any country, even if his realm was largely of the imagination.

"It is a political job; it is a political calling for me to redeem Africa," Garvey stated. "It is like asking Napoleon to take the world. He took a certain portion of the world in his time. He failed and died in St. Helena. But may I not say that the lessons of

Napoleon are but stepping stones by which we shall guide ourselves to African Liberation?"

The Black Napoleon launched the African Redemption Fund. He said most black people would remain in North America at first. They would send their best scientists, mechanics, and artisans ahead to Africa to build the railroads and school systems necessary for when the majority answered the command to "Come Home."

Black Star would soon send the first vessel of black people back to Africa.

★ ★ ★

Critics noted then, as today, that Africa is not a country, but many nations, and that it can be romanticized in the mind of a man like Garvey, who had never actually been there. But he read deeply, including the work of abolitionist Paul Cuffee. Cuffee was an Aquinnah Wampanoag-West Africa Ashanti man who helped resettle freed slaves in Nova Scotia and then in Sierra Leone.

Garvey focused on Liberia, using his connection to the Mayor of Monrovia to deal for land so the soon-coming settlers could grow food. A small advance guard of the UNIA went to Liberia to begin building the new old world.

★ ★ ★

Garvey's mind began to solidify on purely racial lines. He'd been raised in a Jamaica where many dark-skinned people sought out the lighter-skinned people to have lighter children.

"Not all black men are willing to commit race

suicide and to abhor their race for the companionship of another," sneered Garvey, who was once engaged to a Spanish-Irish heiress. "Instead of encouraging a wholesale bastardy in the race, we feel that we should now set out to create a race type and standard of our own."

Like the original Moses, Garvey even helped write the Bible. Shulamith, daughter of Pharaoh and fiancée of Solomon, was previously described as "dark but comely." Garvey rewrote it as "dark and comely."

Illusions of racial purity danced in the air. But Marcus Garvey's great theory already contained the fatal crack that would eventually crush all of his dreams.

Song 11: The Honours of a Disgraced Race

On February 5, 1818, Sir Walter Scott entered Edinburgh Castle to open the treasure chest that had lain undisturbed for a century in the fort's strongroom. The great castle, planted atop an ancient, extinct volcano on a site occupied since the Bronze Age, was rumoured to hold the Honours of Scotland.

The Honours first enter history collectively at the coronation of the infant Mary, Queen of Scots, in 1543. The solid silver Sceptre, surmounted with three figures supporting a crystal globe, held a Scottish pearl on top. Pope Alexander VI gave it to King James IV in 1494.

Pope Julius II handed the metre-long Sword of State to James IV in 1507. The red and gold Crown sat upon the heads of Scotland's monarchs until 1651, when Charles II was crowned king at Scone as the rampaging armies of Oliver Cromwell closed in on him.

Most powerful of all was the Stone of Destiny, a sacred symbol of the Scottish race, a stone on which Scottish kings had been crowned for seven hundred years – including Macbeth.

In the wartorn years following 1651, Scots hid the regalia to keep it out of English hands. Cromwell had already destroyed the English Crown Jewels and planned to do the same thing to the Scottish Honours. The sacred symbols were lowered out of a besieged castle and taken by a serving woman, who smuggled them to a church, where the minister hid them in the bottom of his bed before burying them under the church pulpit. The English occupied the area and the Regalia went on the run again.

Following 1707's Treaty of the Union, wherein the nations of Scotland and England were officially merged, the Regalia vanished for a century. Many Scots thought the English had finally grabbed the Crown Jewels and taken them to London.

By 1818, no one knew where they were, or if they even existed anymore. But Sir Walter Scott had a hunch that they remained in the strongroom of Edinburgh Castle. With the panache of Geraldo Rivera opening Al Capone's vaults on live TV in 1986, Scott staged a high-profile media day where he would enter the castle, open the chest, and discover if the Honours of Scotland remained in Scotland.

★ ★ ★

Scott searched the castle with the smiling approval of the future George IV, the unified ruler of Scotland and England. Just seventy years before, King George II fought off a deadly threat from Charles

Edward Stuart, better known to us as Bonnie Prince Charlie, who invaded England with a conquering Highland Scottish army. Charlie's defeat led to 1746's Pacification of Scotland, where English army divisions raped and murdered their way across the Highlands. Any signs of Scottish culture – kilts, tartans, and swords – were made illegal. People found to have one hidden away in their home were killed on the spot.

Later that century, the Highland Clearances forced Highlanders off their ancient land to be replaced by sheep. The symbolism was potent – the Highlanders were seen as rebels, and so would be replaced by sheep. The clan system was utterly destroyed. The Scottish diaspora fled across the world, including to New Scotland – Nova Scotia.

Highlander culture was deeply stigmatized and most people saw it as a source of shame. That's why Nova Scotia at the time emphasized itself as British, not Highland Scottish.

But by 1818, visionaries like Sir Walter Scott began reclaiming the pride of the Scottish race. Scott, a poet, judge, and president of the Royal Society of Edinburgh, captured attention for his great height and his distinct limp, a legacy of childhood polio. He took pride in his poetry, but wrote his Scottish novels in secret. *Waverley*, published anonymously in 1814, recast the 1745 Jacobite uprising, which culminated in the Battle of Culloden in 1746, as a romantic bid for self-determination by a proud race. Scots loved the novel. Amazingly, so did the English, and a lot of other people, and it became a best-seller. *Rob Roy* followed in 1817, set during the 1715 Jacobite rising, and further building sympathy for the Highlanders.

His novels changed the public mood of Britain. The terrible history of the brutal wars and suppressions between England and Scotland were made safe as heritage. Scott wished to give English minds a way to embrace the Scottish race as a romantic extension of their own identity, and move away from seeing Highlanders as a dangerous, scary, lower race.

On Hogmany 1817 (the Scottish term for New Year's Eve), a giant ship left Edinburgh carrying only one thing: copies of *Rob Roy* for the London market. Europeans were reassessing colonial attitudes and open to seeing their own kings and queens displayed across a wider spectrum of light. The Jacobite resisters were compared favourably to those French who resisted Napoleon, then serving his second exile on the island of St. Helena.

⋆ ⋆ ⋆

The crown jewel in Scott's project to reclaim the racial pride of the Scots was the literal Crown Jewels. And so in the winter of 1818, Scott and a small team of explorers went deep inside Edinburgh Castle and focused their search on a giant oak casket covered in one hundred years of dust.

Scott described his intense eagerness as the workmen used their tools to break into the chest, which gave off a disturbingly hollow sound with each strike. He worried the casket would be empty, and his plan would backfire into Highlander anger that the English had after all found and destroyed the sacred objects, thereby offering "a fair pretext" for breaking the union.

Scott brushed off the dirt and creaked open the

heavy top. "Their joy was therefore extreme when, the ponderous lid having been forced open … the regalia were discovered lying at the bottom covered with linen cloths, exactly as they had been left in 1707," a historian later wrote.

"I have the pleasure to assure you the Regalia of Scotland were this day found in perfect preservation," Scott wrote to an ally. "The extreme solemnity of opening sealed doors of oak and iron, and finally breaking open a chest which had been shut since 7th March 1707," had a profound effect on him.

Scott laid out his plan in a February 7 letter: he wanted the jewels displayed to the public for a small fee. He calculated that seeing the Regalia would "make a pleasant and favourable impression upon them in respect to the kingly part of the constitution."

When I visited Edinburgh Castle a few years ago, I paid a slightly larger fee and saw the Honours of Scotland – the Stone of Destiny, the Sword of State, the Sceptre and the Crown – on display in that very room. (I also took my photo on the castle esplanade, on the patch of Nova Scotian soil where the colony's first baronets were created in the early 1600s.)

In 1822, King George IV visited Scotland and found Edinburgh decorated with tartans and kilts. He paid his respects to the Crown Jewels.

The rehabilitation of the disgraced Scottish race was complete. English minds stopped seeing Scottish people as a dangerous Other that needed to be pushed out of the mainstream of British history, and began to see it as part of the collective identity.

Song 12: Reclaiming the Race

Marcus Garvey decided to reclaim the pride of the black race. His crown jewels were two words: black and Africa. We've seen how he turned black shame into racial pride. He now decided that Africa itself had to be redeemed – at least, the mental construct of the continent did.

Most North Americans saw Africa as an embarrassing continent to be from. People imagined it to be an uncultivated land where slaves could be plucked like berries from a bush. Cartoons of Africans always showed savage cannibals dancing wildly.

Garvey tasted those insults, too, as black and white opponents mocked his self-given titles and ambitious style of dressing. Some people believed evolution applied to human races, and that different colours of people actually represented different kinds of people. Light-skinned people controlled the textbooks, and the textbooks taught that a natural racial hierarchy naturally placed pale people at the top and dark people at the bottom. This world view turned the memory of slavery into a noble one, an effort by the higher race to civilize the lower races.

Garvey's idea attracted a lot of people who feared either that this racial view was true, or that it was a lie of sufficient power to effectively render it the truth.

So it confused everybody when he held a summit with Ku Klux Klan Imperial Wizard Edward Young Clarke in Atlanta, Georgia, in June 1922. The KKK rode high in those days, their membership filled with converts who had seen 1915's *Birth of a Nation* (which screened in the White House), felt its portrayal of heroic white people battling savage black people, and signed up to defend their race.

By the time Garvey visited the Imperial Wizard, the Klan had killed three thousand people, mostly black, since the end of the Civil War. Lynch mobs murdered people because they crossed race lines, or just happened to be nearby.

"Have this day interviewed Edward Young Clarke, acting Imperial Wizard Knight of the Ku Klux Klan. In conference of two hours he outlined the aims and objects of the Klan. He denied any hostility toward the [Universal] Negro Improvement Association," Garvey telegrammed back to Liberty Hall in New York, the headquarters of the association.

"He believes America to be a white man's country, and also states that the Negro should have a country of his own in Africa. He denied that his organization, since its reorganization, ever officially attacked the Negro. He has been invited to speak at forthcoming convention to further assure the race of the stand of the Klan."

Garvey saw a potential partnership between his black rights movement and the KKK's goals. Both sides wanted Africans in the Americas to go back to Africa. Why not work together? He added that the Imperial Wizard would be invited to buy stock in Black Star Line. Garvey never explained away those three thousand lynch murders.

Few of his followers saw the KKK as potential friends. The leading black journal *The Messenger* wrote, "Garvey, Black Eagle, Becomes Messenger Boy for Clarke, Ku Klux Keagle." Ouch.

The North American journal reminded its readers that Garvey was from Jamaica, and so had different ideas about the world. It fired "the opening gun in a campaign to drive Garvey and Garveyism in all its sinister viciousness from the American soil."

★ ★ ★

Fading fans of Garvey's joked that his Africa for Africans campaign had morphed into America for Whites, and that he was abandoning African-American rights in America. A statement attributed to Garvey raced around the country.

"This is a white man's country. He found it, he conquered it, and we can't blame him if he wants to keep it. I am not vexed with the white man of the South for Jim Crowing me because I am black. I never built any street cars or railroads. The white man built them for his own conveniences. And if I don't want to ride where he's willing to ride, then I'd better walk," he allegedly said.

His enemies almost certainly wrote that and lied

to attribute it to him, but it spread widely and tarnished his brand, making him seem a man in rapid retreat, not a man forwarding his generation.

The National Association for the Advancement of Colored People (NAACP) called Garvey a "Negro of unmixed stock, squat, stocky, fat and sleek, with protruding jaws and heavy jowls, small bright pig-like eyes and a rather bull-dog like face. Boastful, egotistic, tyrannical, intolerant, cunning, shifty, smooth and suave, avaricious."

Garvey dismissed his rival W.E.B. Du Bois as a "lazy dependent mulatto" and a hater of dark people. Du Bois, finding some calm, reflected that the put-down contained a "kernel of truth that gains him his following; there are plenty of black folk who are bitterly ashamed of their color."

J. Edgar Hoover, the secretly gay and openly paranoid head of the FBI, increased his spying activity against Garvey, whom he called the "notorious Negro agitator," and pressed his government to prosecute Garvey and put him in jail.

★ ★ ★

Garvey fought back with Colonel Hubert Fauntleroy Julian, the first black pilot in the western hemisphere, roaring in to land at Liberty Hall in a biplane. The gorgeous, charismatic aviator reminded people of what Garvey believed he stood for: black pride. So did Brave Bessie Coleman, the first woman black pilot, who backed Garvey with her magnificent calm.

But rumours swirled that Garvey would be assassinated at the Universal Negro Improvement

Association summer convention. As Hoover pressed in from the secret parts of the federal government, and black rivals degraded his standing in the newspapers, Garvey tried to find the centre. He failed. Instead, he shocked the faithful by abruptly resigning as leader of the UNIA and as provisional President of Africa.

A writer at *The Messenger* received a human hand in the mail, accompanied by a threat to send his own hand on to someone else. It was signed as being from the KKK, and interpreted as the KKK sticking up for Garvey. Garvey swore he had nothing to do with it.

Speaking in New Orleans in 1922, Garvey ignored death threats and took the stage with the mayor and police chief. A huge crowd listened to him berate the mayor to his face; the police chief rose and threatened to arrest Garvey. Audley Moore, a famous African-American civil rights leader known as Queen Mother Moore, captured the scene.

"When he did this, everybody jumped up on benches and pulled out their guns and just held the guns in the air and said, 'Speak, Garvey, speak.' And Garvey said, 'As I was saying,' and he went on and repeated what he had said before, and the police filed out of the hall like little puppy dogs with their tails behind them," she wrote.

Garvey talked his way out of trouble. People called his oration thunder from heaven, entrancing words that stirred souls and echoed in the secret chambers of hearts.

★ ★ ★

A prominent critic of Garvey's, Rev. James Eason, was assassinated in 1923. Many accused Garvey of having a role in the killing; Garvey said it was not true. "We are not willing to go so far as to say that Marcus Garvey was implicated directly or indirectly in the cowardly assassination of J.W.H. Eason," wrote the *New York Amsterdam News*. "The men who actually shot Mr. Eason may have thought they were doing the UNIA a service, but they are mistaken. What they actually did was to give it its first serious blow – a blow from which it will never, never recover."

The Black Star Line finally hit the financial reefs and sank. In the swirling chaos, the government built a case against Garvey, accusing him of mail fraud. Garvey acted as his own lawyer. He lost his case and the jury convicted him of sending out advertisements through the post, encouraging investors to buy shares in the shipping company while he already knew the shares would be worthless. He was sent to the Manhattan Detention Center. Ironically, it was called the Tombs prison because the site had originally housed a building designed like an Egyptian mausoleum. The provisional president of Africa found himself imprisoned in an American imitation of Egypt.

In June 1923, the judge sentenced him to five years in jail. One newspaper wrote it was "too bad. The distinguished son of Ethiopia makes the world more interesting than before he came. To jail Marcus Garvey would dim romance, like jailing a rainbow."

But the state locked that rainbow behind bars.

* * *

After three months, he got bail and returned to a celebration at Liberty Hall. He resumed his work and new recruits swelled to hear his accounts of his martyrdom. He announced plans for the Black Cross Navigation and Trading Company, a new Black Star Line. It would set sail, he said, in the fall, bringing colonists to Liberia. Later that year, the "vanguard of African Redemption" sailed for Liberia. Garvey stayed in America and raised money – his goal was $2 million – to fund the colony.

But his Liberian dream died when the Liberian president soundly rejected him. "No person or persons leaving the U.S. under the auspices of the Garvey movement in the U.S. will be allowed to land in the republic of Liberia," the government said in a press release.

Garvey wanted to go back to Africa, but it seemed Africa did not want him. The UNIA colonists returned to the U.S. Garvey was sent back to jail.

* * *

In February 1925, Marcus Garvey re-entered the federal penitentiary as the most famous black prisoner in the world. He became prisoner 19359, and that number soon became the most sought after in Harlem's street lottery.

He wrote powerful letters from prison, reviving a tradition dating back to Saint Paul. "When I am dead wrap the mantle of the Red Black and Green around me, for in the new life I shall rise with God's grace and blessings to lead the millions up the heights of triumph with the colours that you well know," he wrote.

"Look for me in the whirlwind or the storm, look for me all around you, for, with God's grace, I shall come and bring with me countless millions of black slaves who have died in America and the West Indies and the millions in Africa to aid you in the fight for liberty, freedom and life."

He continued to write for *Negro World*, the magazine he founded. "The time has come for the Negro to forget and cast behind him his hero worship and adoration of other races," he wrote in an important editorial called African Fundamentalism. "We must inspire a literature and promulgate a doctrine of our own … When we were embracing the arts and sciences on the banks of the Nile, their ancestors were still drinking human blood and eating out of the skulls of their conquered dead."

His thinking had taken on a markedly black and white tone. Compliments to the black race paired with insults to the white race. He now dreamed of founding a "racial empire whose only natural, spiritual and political aims shall be God and Africa, at home and abroad."

★ ★ ★

Earnest Cox, author of *White America*, also studied the African diaspora, but not for reasons of liberty. He wanted to see how others controlled black people and concluded that Garvey's idea of a return to Africa would solve what he saw as America's Negro problem. The two exchanged letters and a friend of Cox visited Garvey in prison.

Garvey also found intellectual companionship in ancient Rome, reading *The Meditations of Marcus Aurelius*, which inspired his *The Meditations of Marcus Garvey*. In 1927, he wrote a prison poem in the style of

Oscar Wilde, calling it "The White Man's Game, His Vanity Fair."

He wrote to U.S. President Calvin Coolidge seeking early release. He bolstered his case with letters from nine of the ten jurors who had convicted him. UNIA members wrote to the government, too, including a man called Earl Little. Little told the president that releasing Garvey would be his "priceless gift to the Negro … causing his name to be honoured with generations yet unborn." Garvey had visited Little at home in better days, and likely met his son, Malcolm. The son would later drop the last name Little in favour of the letter X.

In Detroit, Garveyites held a silent parade, and Garveyites from across the continent pressed for his release. "Behind his sordid, somber prison's walls, this black man with Napoleonic vision sits crushed in body and mind," wrote the *Chicago Whip* newspaper. "The glint of steel that once burned in his eyes is fading out and he sits, thin and emaciated, gazing always forward with a faraway stare."

The Attorney General John Sargent wrote to President Coolidge suggesting he consider early release, and also explaining that "the prosecution was designed for the protection of colored people." But the colored people rallied to Garvey, not the government, and saw it not as the just penalty for breaking the law, but "as an act of oppression of the race." On November 18, 1927, Coolidge agreed to free Garvey – on the condition that he instantly be deported from the U.S. Two years and nine months after he was locked up, Garvey was duly released from prison and put straight onto a ship exiling him from his adopted homeland.

On December 3, 1927, Garvey donned a brown checked suit, picked up his silver-topped malacca cane, and crossed the plank to the ship at the Mississippi docks. Some one thousand supporters gathered to see him off.

"I leave America fully as happy as when I came, in that my relationship with the Negro people was most pleasant and inspiring. My entire life will be devoted to the support of the cause. I sincerely believe that it is only by nationalizing the Negro and awakening him to the possibilities of himself that his universal problem can be solved," he said.

The ship steamed down the Mississippi; Garvey stood on the deck waving to miles and miles of supporters grief-struck that he was leaving.

Virginia Collins was there. "People in general, they was just waving, waving, waving and crying and waving, because it was just like you was losing your own, or losing yourself. What are we going to do now? That was uppermost in people's thoughts."

It was probably topmost of Garvey's thoughts, too.

★ ★ ★

Over the next decade, Garvey would walk a profound spiritual journey, taking him to the mountaintop – or at least to Sydney, Nova Scotia – that inspired him to write his redemption song.

First, though, let's look at that fatal flaw in Garvey's thinking. He took great pride in his African roots and the black race. But it turns out we're all black people.

Song 13:
The Curiosity Advantage

In 1647, the Protestant Primate of All Ireland, James Ussher, figured out when the world began. By counting backwards through the Bible, he concluded that Creation began at about 6 p.m. on October 22, 4004 B.C. It was an incredible academic achievement built on decades of study.

He turned out to be off the mark. Scientists now calculate the age of the Earth at 4.5 billion years.

Christianity got a lot of science wrong. The universe isn't a small, static dome over our heads; it's infinitely huge and expanding in all directions at 68 kilometres per second per megaparsec. (The scientific papers I consulted describe that as "really fast.")

Human beings weren't crafted out of dirt and ribs by a deity; we evolved from earlier animals.

But Christianity got it spot on with one scientific fact: Adam fathered the entire human race, and Eve is mother to us all.

Geneticists have traced the Y chromosome (handed down from father to son only) back about 130,000 years, and by studying mutations tracked "Adam" back to the Rift Valley in today's Ethiopia.

The same work takes us back perhaps 200,000 years to mitcochondrial Eve, the most recent matrilineal ancestor to all the women on Earth.

Adam and Eve thought differently. They looked at the raw materials of the world and found better ways to create hunting weapons and tools. Adam taught his brothers and sons how to stalk prey. Eve learned unprecedented ways to gather food.

Eve and Adam used their mental advantage to become the ultimate superancestors. Their curiosity advantage swept through the small human world. About five thousand families separate Adam's time from ours. Five thousand pairs of parents raising children. A small town's population equals the short time trip from our common great ancestors to us.

Humanity held little territory back then. Most of Africa was in the hands of other animals. The rest of the world was almost entirely human-free.

Adam, with his brothers and sons, fought off lions and rival tribes, supplementing his family's diet of gathered berries and nuts with what they killed, scrabbling forward while protecting his family. Adam probably died young, by our standards. But he did enough to get his son into adulthood.

Eve birthed her children on the savannah, protecting and providing for them as they grew old enough to have their own children. She taught them new ways of surviving in the harsh world. She taught them to rise as kings and queens over the animal kingdom.

Ethiopia stretched out her hands unto God.

Language might not have existed when Adam and Eve walked the Earth, so there's a good chance Adam and Eve communicated in sounds and gestures. They had fire, tools, and probably clothes, and in most respects were genetically identical to modern people. The entire human population lived in northeast Africa, and numbered 10,000.

What colour were they?

★ ★ ★

DNA and archeology show that "anatomically modern" humans walked the Earth at least 200,000 years ago, and maybe 276,000 years ago. The bones and tools found in Ethiopia show an animal waking up to her own consciousness and regarding the world through new eyes. It shows a species of animal trying to emancipate itself from the animal kingdom.

Back then, there really were different species of humanity. Neanderthals ruled Europe and central Asia from 200,000 years ago to 40,000 years ago. Homo floresiensis (a.k.a. the Hobbit) lived in modern Indonesia at least 94,000 years ago and the last person died 18,000 years ago. People we call the Denisovans lived in Siberia and parts of Asia until about 40,000 years ago.

But every other branch of humans died out, leaving only one survivor: Homo sapiens. Us.

★ ★ ★

Humans were originally either pale or dark, depending on how you define "originally."

Millions of years ago, when Lucy and her ape sisters came down from the trees to walk the savannah, black fur covered our chalk-white skin But proto-humans with less hair got an evolutionary advantage. Less fur meant you could cool down quicker. Soon, the genetic advantage spread and proto-humans lost most of their fur, apart from patches on the head, genitals, and a light coat covering most of their frame.

But white skin burns easily under African sun and soon darker-skinned people found they had an evolutionary boost. Under the hot African sun, humanity turned black.

If you're an Amangu woman reading this in southwest Australia, a Nordic man in Finland, or a Korean in Seoul, we all looked the same back then. We know that about 200,000 years ago, humanity was one black ethnic group living in Africa.

About 60,000 years ago, people lived in small groups. Climate change, drought, comet strikes, and volcanoes nearly killed the last of the humans. But our ancestors survived.

They developed language and that powered their expansion across Africa and into the modern Middle East. Geographic obstacles like mountains, rivers, oceans, and deserts separated the different groups, just as it does with all animals and plants. But even today, all of us are 99.9 per cent biochemically identical.

Bands crossed the Gates of Grief (or Bab-al-Mandab Strait) into modern Yemen, and followed the beaches of coastal India to Southeast Asia. By 45,000 years ago, they had settled Indonesia and Papua New

Guinea, with stationary groups growing more alike while new branches kept breaking off to expand into the next plot of land. By 50,000 years ago, one group of pioneers sailed all the way to Australia.

Everybody still looked more or less the same – modern Aboriginal people in Australia probably look most like people did way back then. That's because they found themselves genetically isolated from their cousins on the main Eurasian landmass and so changed less.

By about 40,000 years ago, a second group left Africa and migrated inland over the generations, passing through the Middle East into Central Asia. From this base camp, they colonized northern Asia, Europe, and beyond. By 35,000 years ago, humans lived widely in Europe alongside Neanderthals, who slowly disappeared until extinction about 25,000 years ago. Some Neanderthal people and Homo sapien people had children together, and many non-African people have a small amount of Neanderthal DNA in them.

About 20,000 years ago, as *National Geographic* describes it, a small band of these people turned into the "face of the storm" during the Last Glacial Maximum and crossed a land bridge connecting the Old World to the New World. They navigated the great glaciers to populate the Americas and become today's First Nations.

Tribes of people started to look different from each other. When humans live near the equator, they tend to stay dark-skinned. When they migrate away from the equator, people with paler skin get an evolutionary advantage by letting more vitamin C into the skin in sun-starved areas. So northern and southern people – Europeans and Chinese and Inuit – turn pale.

* * *

Online research into human racial groups leads you to white power websites and sociology papers proclaiming that it's all a social construction.

Both are wrong.

A 2002 study at the University of Southern California and Stanford fed details of a sample of people from around the world into a computer and it sorted them into five groups, based on closest genetic similarity.

It reported that by 40,000 years ago the "divergent evolutionary branching out" produced five regions of humans. The computer (and other research) found you can trace all modern humans back to these groups representing their continent of origin. They are:

1. The Congoid of southern Africa
2. The Capoid of sub-Saharan Africa
3. The Australoid of India, Southeast Asia, Indonesia, New Guinea, and Australia
4. The Mongoloid of Northeast Asia
5. The Caucasoid of Europe, North Africa, and West Asia.

Where are white people and black people? The computer can't see skin colour, which essentially means colour-coded systems are mental mistakes. White people, please note: we belong to the Caucasoid group of Europe, North Africa, and West Asia.

If you retrace the ancestral steps from Kenya to Norway, you won't cross a border where people turn from black to white. Instead, you'll see a slow transformation of features. The same thing happens whichever direction you travel.

People lost touch with their relatives, as we all do, what with the melting glaciers reflooding the land bridge from Turtle Island to Russia and cutting the First Nations off from the rest of the world 12,000 years ago, people getting stranded in Australia even further back than that, and mountains, grand rivers, lakes, and oceans reshaping behind the migrants to isolate them in their new homes.

But we were still all black.

The people who painted the cave art in Lascaux, France, 17,300 years ago were black Europeans. Recent genetic studies on 7,000-year-old human remains in Spain showed they were still black then.

"The biggest surprise was to discover that this individual possessed African versions in the genes that determine light pigmentation of the current Europeans, which indicates that he had dark skin," scientist Carles Lalueza-Fox told CBC News in January 2014.

Oh – and he probably had blue eyes.

"It seems increasingly likely that the modern races formed mainly in the Holocene, after twelve to ten thousand years ago," writes anthropologist Richard Klein.

About 10,000 years ago, the end of the Last Glacial Maximum saw human skulls change around the world as people became more gracile, or slender, probably because we became less aggressive animals.

Northern peoples started to pale. Dark skin keeps the sun's vitamin D out of humans, so the change may have let more vitamin D in the lands of long, lightless winters. It was a reverse of the earlier post-fur shift from pale skin to dark.

Despite the superficial changes, when humanity's distant branches rediscovered each other in the 1500s, we found we could all still make more humans. An Australoid man from Australia can marry a Caucasoid woman from Norway and create beautiful babies. We are still the same species, all from Ethiopia, with some adaptations to local conditions.

But that's not what we thought. And that's when things took a turn for the ugly. In Song 15, we'll learn about the invention of racism.

Song 14:
Back to Africa

Crowds mobbed Marcus Garvey when he returned to Jamaica in December 1927. He climbed on top of a car and preached.

"They dragged me through the streets of Harlem like a common thief," he cried. "But oh, thou God of Ethiopia, who when the Assyrians spat on thee and Jews jeered thee, remember, it was Simon of Cyrenia, a Negro, who helped you to bear your cross. Can you forget the Negro now?"

Through the common lens of their Christianity, Garvey made his individual misfortune part of the universal pain.

Vivian Durham, a Garveyite who welcomed him home, said when Garvey's trumpet sounded, it pulled down the walls the people had built around their suffering. Grown men cried freely. When the UNIA anthem lifted from the brass band, thousands of lungs pushed the song of freedom into the air.

"We may have a problem on our hands," worried *The Gleaner*, the newspaper of the comfortable.

From his island stronghold, Garvey plotted his next move toward emancipation.

Restless Garvey sailed to Europe in the first half of 1928 and found a sympathetic white audience backing his idea of Africa for the Africans. The British government, however, barred him from the colonies and discouraged him from the Commonwealth.

He returned to Canada, landing in Montreal in November. Police quickly arrested him and his second wife, Amy Jacques. (They had married in 1922, shortly after his divorce from Amy Ashwood.)

The couple was jailed overnight before the "misunderstanding" was cleared up. Canadians spread rumours that he was planning to use Montreal as a base for attacking America. "Canada shall not be used as a base for the purpose of the attack of neighbouring countries," warned the *Montreal Gazette*.

Officials told Garvey he could stay in Canada so long as he stayed silent in public. He travelled to Toronto and Hamilton. In Hamilton, armed soldiers and police stopped him from entering the city and forced him back onto the ship.

The Garveys returned to Jamaica, but he ran into more hostility. He was convicted of "demeaning the judiciary and undermining public confidence in them" and slung into a Jamaican jail. From his prison cell, his writing in *Blackman* brought him another six-month sentence, this time for contempt. While legally dubious, it's pretty clear that contempt is exactly what he felt for the power-brokers who tried to kill his ideas by arresting his tongue and pen.

Spies followed him, reporting his words and warning his "speeches are and will have a disturbing effect among people and if kept up will lead to riot and bloodshed."

In 1930, he got good news: Marcus Garvey Junior, born September 17, and then a second boy, Julius, in 1933.

★ ★ ★

The UNIA halls in Glace Bay, Whitney Pier, and New Waterford saw steady growth in the 1920s, gathering the community under the banner of One God! One Aim! One Destiny! The halls served as cultural and community centres, hosting weddings and wakes. They often held concerts, and it wasn't unusual for white families to come over to enjoy the music.

The halls were built by the men, who donated their time, and paid for by membership dues. A portion of that money also went to the UNIA headquarters in the U.S. to further Garvey's work.

Sydney's hall in Whitney Pier opened in 1919 with 250 members, but by 1929 the community realized it needed to reboot. It did so with a fresh slate of people: George Lucas as president, Alonzo Lucas as vice-president, W.E. Smith as vice-president, Conrod Hayes as secretary, and Julian Brewster as treasurer. It also boasted a thirty-five-member marching band.

The New Waterford Hall opened in 1929. Alan Hamilton, a prominent black lawyer and publisher, spoke at the opening. He praised the "men of action who had a vision … men who were striving to leave something behind."

Garveyites in Nova Scotia also started the African

Orthodox Church (AOC) and Garvey himself asked Reverend George Alexander McGuire to be its chaplain. McGuire became the AOC's first bishop in 1921.

The UNIA halls doubled as churches for the small black community, although many also belonged to the Anglican All Saints Church. Many black people worshipped at St. Alban's Church in Whitney Pier, but had to stand because all the pews were rented to white members of the congregation. This led many black Christians to switch to the AOC.

As the UNIA faded during Garvey's time in prison, the Cape Breton members restructured the organization and renamed it the Negro Social Club.

Albert Francis started the Glace Bay hall with a building on his own land in 1918. Francis came from Barbados in 1916 to work in the coal mines of Cape Breton. The organization later opened a new hall on Jessome Street in 1923. Francis had little formal education, but, like Garvey, taught himself a tremendous amount. He wanted a prouder, better day for his black friends and family, and saw the UNIA as a vehicle to do that. He helped organize a New Glasgow UNIA branch.

★ ★ ★

Restless Marcus Garvey toured Jamaica to see what the Great Depression was doing to his people. Life for the poor was worse than it was in the days after slavery ended. He fought to improve their lives by haranguing politicians who otherwise ignored them.

One such politician, wrote Garvey, "put forward the most grotesque proposals for the improvement of the human race and Jamaica in particular, which could not bear even looking into, still less encouraging."

But you can't turn back a tsunami with stern letters. Garvey sourced his power not in himself, but in his people.

Poverty bit his own family, and his wife and children struggled to get by. Garvey nearly lost his house and got into legal trouble for failing to pay taxes. The water company cut him off. The Black Napoleon found himself marooned on his very own St. Helena. He spurned offers to work with officials, to operate in a colour-coded world, and to thus escape poverty. Finally, he sold his worldly belongings and did what he always did. When spring bloomed in 1935, he left Jamaica.

His family stayed behind, hoping to join him in better times.

"I left Jamaica a broken man, broken in spirit, broken in health, and broken in pocket," he lamented. "I will never, never go back."

⋆ ⋆ ⋆

Once, Garvey paraded the streets of New York as the President of Africa; now he ambled aimlessly along London's cobblestones, wondering where the people had gone. "Sometimes I long for peace, but where could I find it?" he wrote.

The flirtation with the KKK drove many away, never to return. The mood of Ireland for the Irish and Africa for the Africans faded from the global stage as Nazi Germany and Imperial Japan sought to conquer independent nations and bring them into their empires.

Garvey got a new stepladder and began climbing it again, now in Hyde Park's Speaker's Corner. He could still draw a crowd and silence a heckler. "He has a great stock of humour – I did not know it before – by which he ridiculed many an interrupter into embarrassing silence," wrote Grenadian journalist and political activist T.A. Marryshow.

In Jamaica, his absence made the press grow fonder. The newspapers that once mocked him for what they saw as pretentious overreaching now reported that Britain's Labour Party had recruited him as a star candidate for the Mother of all Parliaments.

That would have made him Britain's first black MP, but it was just a rumour that wafted away.

★ ★ ★

As his death approached, Garvey stooped his aging body, picked up the worn-out tools, and rebuilt. He wrote. He published. He spoke. He attacked the portrayal of black people in popular culture, as they alternated between Noble Savage, ugly brute, and subservient wild thing, but rarely as an individual human.

Garvey fell out of the collective mind. He was no longer the most famous black person around. A black actor, athlete, and singer named Paul Robeson became more famous than Garvey, and above both of them towered an actual African ruler, the man named Haile Selassie, emperor of Ethiopia.

You'll recall that in 1916, Garvey left Jamaica with the prophecy that one day a black prince would rise in Africa to redeem the black race. In 1930, Ethiopia's Selassie was crowned black emperor of a black country on a black continent. Garvey celebrated his coronation at first.

"The Psalmist prophesied that Princes would come out of Egypt and Ethiopia would stretch forth her hands unto God. We have no doubt that the time is now come. Ethiopia is now really stretching forth her hands. This great kingdom of the East has been hidden for many centuries, but gradually she is rising to take a leading place in the world and it is for us of the Negro race to assist in every way to hold up the hand of the Emperor Ras Tafari," he wrote in the November 8, 1930, edition of *Blackman.*

In 1935, deepening the biblical imagery, the Beast of Rome attacked as Mussolini invaded Ethiopia.

Before his coronation, Selassie was known by the title Ras Tafari. In the Ethiopian language Amharic, *ras* means head or prince and *tafari* means he who inspires awe.

After his coronation, many saw him as the black messiah the Negro world had waited for. Imagine it: a black king fighting off a white dictator. It thrilled Garvey deeply. A famous photo showed Ras Tafari standing with one foot on an Italian bomb. Black rebels sailed to Ethiopia to fight in the resistance.

Garvey abandoned his early admiration for Selassie as he lost battle after battle to the Italians. European armies marched into Abyssinia, conquering one of the last free African countries.

On May 4, 1936, Selassie fled Addis Ababa for Jerusalem and then London. Melbourne's *Argus* newspaper reported on the evacuation, saying, "It is generally believed that organized resistance is at an end."

"Haile Selassie's flight was a startling and unexpected development," the reporter wrote. "Only a few hours before the news was announced he had made a dramatic appeal for a last stand in defence of the capital, and had told newspaper correspondents that he would never surrender."

Before he left, Selassie and his wife opened the palace doors and invited ordinary people in to take what they could carry. They did so, carting off beds, carpets, clothes, and weapons.

Marcus Garvey brought a UNIA delegation to meet the defeated messiah at London's Waterloo Station. Selassie walked by them without a glance. Garvey, tired and disillusioned, turned against his former great black hope, calling him a "feudal monarch who looks down upon his slaves and serfs with contempt."

* * *

Many of Ethiopia's ruling elite felt they were actually white people and saw themselves as racially superior to the black people who held them up as black kings. Garvey believed this was true of Selassie, a "great coward who ran away from his country to save his skin and left the millions of his countrymen to struggle through a terrible war."

Really, how did it even occur to Bob Marley and the Rastafarians to link these two?

Many Garveyites failed to see the logic in attacking the emperor, and instead Garvey's words drove his people further from him. Imagine the barber shop conversations as defenders of Garvey explained how it made sense to speak fondly of the KKK while denouncing the black emperor. Few could bridge the gap, and people ignored his stepladder oratory. "The halo around St. Marcus's head is rapidly growing faint, and with it Negro nationalism. The figure of

Emperor Haile Selassie, commanding the intense admiration and support of all racial groups, gives the Negro his first vision of internationalism," wrote George Padmore, a Marxist Pan-Africanist.

Garvey, restless once more, stirred again, boarding a ship to cross the Atlantic in the dying days of peaceful waters. He brought his ideas to Canada, hoping to raise funds for UNIA, and relight the extinguished flame. He spoke at Toronto, delivering his School of African Philosophy. Then, the tired man pulled himself hundreds of miles east, to Nova Scotia.

* * *

Marcus Garvey arrived in Menelik Hall in Sydney, Nova Scotia, on October 1, 1937. The meeting opened with music. Garvey took his seat on the stage next to Mayor S.E Muggah, the Reverend James Ford, pastor of St. Philip's African Orthodox Church, and other dignitaries. For the people who had founded and nurtured the UNIA in Nova Scotia, it was a time of tremendous excitement.

The reverend introduced Garvey.

"We extend greetings to you from the City of Sydney and Cape Breton. In the person of the Honourable Marcus Garvey we have a man of the race who is conscious of his task. In him we have a captain at the helm," Ford said.

The mayor extended a cordial welcome. "The colored colony in this city is one of which you may well be proud. All you have to do is look and see this hall that they have built for themselves and it is theirs and theirs alone," he said. "The object lesson to be drawn, therefore, is that while granting to the community the same rights, you should stick together in forwarding your own race. If you do that there is no limit to which you will not reach."

Garvey took the stage to sustained applause. He expressed delight at his first visit to Nova Scotia and acknowledged the members of the audience with whom he had corresponded. He noted that black Nova Scotians were greatly outnumbered by whites.

"Indeed, they are a minority and a small minority at that. I hope we will all realize it. Minorities wherever they should happen to find themselves should unite because they are in the midst of a majority. The temper of the majority cannot always be guaranteed, even with the best government," he began.

He pointed to the mounting suffering of minorities in Germany as exemplar of the extreme dangers an outnumbered people faced in their world. "Minorities must be very thoughtful living in the midst of majorities. Your conduct must be such as to leave no loophole to constitute you are an annoyance to the majority, as to give the people of the majority the idea that you are not the people to be in their midst. Alien minorities are always at a disadvantage because they are not in their homeland. We have our homes and we have one principal home, and that home is Africa," he said, his voice settling into his famous staccato rhythm.

"We are radicals, though, in connection with our country. We want to restore our country to its ancient glory. We are seeking to restore the land of our fathers. We came here not by our will – we were pulled here. We had a terrible time in those early days. We did our bit under difficult circumstances here to build up the glory of the race that enslaved us at the time. We contributed a lot to that civilization. If for nothing else that race owes us a lot."

He paused to read his audience, then continued.

"We think there is no better country available to help us than Canada. Canada has always played a fair game. Canada is conscious of the wrong that was imposed upon us to help build up the civilization of which Canada is part. We were brought to lay the prop of the present civilization. We toiled for it. Cane, sugar, rum, cotton were the industries on which the present civilization was built. We carried the load upon our shoulders. If a picture were to be shown as to how the present civilization was built, you will find the Negro holding it up."

Garvey praised Sydney for "giving the Negro a chance."

"The UNIA realizes that it has a responsibility not only to the group, but to the world at large to place the Negro in his proper place," he said. "We are not using any pistols where we are. I do not know if in the whole of Sydney you will find five pistols among the Negroes. I believe you will find more Bibles and prayer books than pistols. Whether with or without pistols, the Negro is looking for his place in the world."

He spoke of meeting Prime Minister Mackenzie King in 1928 at the League of Nations, and how King "has ever been a good friend to our cause."

"Scientists said once that the Negro was the missing link, but now they realize that the Negro is the oldest man in creation. He is so old that he is black, and everything darkens by age, therefore he could not be the missing link."

He cited the great black achievements: building the Pyramids, and the Sphinx; birthing the first civilizations from the Nile to the Congo Basin; the first cultures of the world in Timbuktu, Benin, and Alexandria. From there, civilization spread to Europe and China. He believed it was carried by black men, just as white men sought to conquer the world in his day. But it fell, as all civilizations do.

It was a haunting message to hear in 1937. A few weeks later, Adolf Hitler would hold a secret conference at the Reich Chancellery in Berlin to lay out his plans to seize Czechoslovakia and Austria before invading Poland.

"I should like to see black and white get on so well together that the black man will remember how kind he was. It is the only way we are going to get along because man is man for that. The white man is no missing link, nor the black man, nor the yellow man either," Garvey said.

He paused, and then soared his rhetoric. "We are men whether we are white, yellow or black, because we have one origin. We came from the same place and we are going back to the same place. The Negro went to sleep for a long while, resting from his labours, but he slept too long, so everybody stole a march on him and therefore he is the only man without a country," he said. "Economically, for his own interest, the white man will not like it, but deep down in his heart he will say that the Negro is right."

Garvey stormed on into the night. He spoke about economic growth as key to freedom. "I would like to see Canada for the Canadians, England for the English, America for the Americans, and in the same way I want to see Africa for the Africans, those at home and those abroad, so that when we are sick and tired and weary we may lay our heads in the laps of our mother and ask her to comfort us and bless us before we die."

He reached the mountaintop and saw his vision of the Promised Land: "We are going to emancipate ourselves from mental slavery because whilst others might free the body, none but ourselves can free the mind.

"Mind is your only ruler, sovereign. The man who is not able to develop and use his mind is bound to be the slave of the other man, who uses his mind, because man is related to man under all circumstances for good or ill. If man is not able to protect himself from the other man, he should use his mind to good advantage.

"The fool will always pay the price. The fool will always carry the heavy burden. The fool will always be crushed without a tear from God or man because God Almighty never made a fool. God is all wise. When God Almighty made man in his own image and likeness, it wasn't the physical, it was the mind that was like God. God has his unitary intelligence. When man abuses that intelligence, he lowers himself."

Garvey spoke of the need to lay a foundation today for future generations to grow on. Build ships, or the next generation must always walk.

Exhausted, he finished his speech and sat down to applause.

★ ★ ★

Garvey left Sydney for Halifax. He spoke there on October 7, 1937. Oral history says he gave the speech in Africville. Robert Hill, the great Jamaican Garvey scholar, places it in Bethel Church. The church at 5406 Roome Street sits in the north end of Halifax, a mile or so outside of Africville's 1937 boundaries, but well within its traditional territory, which may explain the apparent discrepancy. And it's a certainty that much of the congregation came from Africville, one of Canada's oldest black communities.

The Halifax Explosion had only happened twenty years earlier. Roome Street was at the centre of the destruction. Africville, less seriously hit by the blast, was entering a long, less obvious ruination. In the days after the explosion, people from around the world sent money to rebuild the wastelands of north-end Halifax. City planners put a map on the table and marked out the reconstruction zone. At first, it included Africville. But at some point, the city redrew the zone and excluded Africville.

Money poured into the North End and Richmond quickly rose from the ashes. Garvey saw signs of rebirth all around him as he walked to the church. But he, like so many others visiting Halifax, would have seen a difference in Africville. It had been stalled in 1917, starved of city funds. They paid their taxes, but didn't get the services.

Many Africville women worked in the North End as nannies and saw the growing discrepancy daily. Where once the working-class white North End and working-class black Africville enjoyed similar civic services, albeit on the low end, reconstruction money lifted white north end out of poverty, but left black

Africville behind.

In the shadow of his approaching death, Garvey spoke to these people. He admitted his visit came as the result of an accident – that his tour of the British West Indies had been delayed, so here he was. He acknowledged the second-class citizenship given to black people, but harangued his audience to accept that and move beyond it.

"It is very unfortunate that such a condition should exist, but such will exist all over the world among the majority of people simply because the majority have been unfortunate not to discover themselves as individuals and people. There are two classes of men in the world – those who succeed, and those who do not succeed," he said.

"One who is critical would be tempted to ask how could they be the same people if they are men who succeed and men who do not succeed. Why this difference? If there were not something personal causing the lack of success and success, then the failure of the individual, the failure of the people, would be attributed to some unkind power who unkindly rules the destiny of these people who failed, and some partial power that rules the destiny of those who succeed."

He reasoned that if this was the case, then that entity would explain differences among people.

"I do not know of such a superior being who is responsible for the existence of man as to make some people succeed and some fail," he added.

These are confusing words, given that he believed in God and spoke in a Christian church. Further still, he had studied racial oppression his entire life, but it seemed to have left his mind. Perhaps shackles still chained his mind, chafing him, making him angry.

"I know of one superior being who is God and surely God could not be so unfair," he clarified, answering the question he must have seen in the faces of those listening to him.

"It is a fact that man fails because of himself and not because of the favour or disfavour of anyone outside of him," Garvey told them. "Every man who fails in life contributes to his own failure and neither God nor man is responsible for that failure."

He ripped into people for being indolent, careless, and uninterested in self-discovery.

"God only made one type of men and that was man. He never made several types of men. He made Adam as a man and God has not interfered with his structure. He has left him from the Garden of Eden until this church at Halifax, a free sovereign creature having in his own hand his own destiny, his own career, and if he messes it up and becomes a crawling being to be trampled by other men, so long will he go on crawling and God will pass him by without even pity," he preached.

You can see why oral history would also add that the white power-holders of Halifax enjoyed Garvey's speech, but Africvillians felt less moved.

He moved onto race, saying first that those who master the world "receive the compliment" of God, and that God blesses them to use the world and occupy it as they see fit. "I represent a race that has come upon the stage of action to understand what the responsibility of man is, and what the responsibility of life is, and so we find ourselves environed by a lawless set of men who have built up tremendous systems in this civilization," he called out in his short, sharp cadences. He pointed to education systems, social systems, religious systems.

"And so we think of the English and French as successful races, as also the Germans, the Italians, the Russians, the Americans and comparatively, we must admit and think the Negro is a failing race. Comparatively, we have done nothing with God's world."

How did these words hit the minds of his audience? Africville people knew then as they do today that their ancestors had physically built Halifax and that until recently Africville's rolling farmlands had helped feed the city, especially during the Great Depression. They knew they worked and paid taxes, but got no running water, no paved streets, no honest policing, and no fire department. They knew that if they were failing, it was because the game was rigged against them.

But Garvey didn't see it that way.

Garvey dug into his argument, challenging them to name a black empire, a black art, a black science, a black business. "Nowhere! And not only in Halifax you will find the Negro poor, incapable to do it for himself, but everywhere he goes he must be dependent on someone else, although he has in him the same pedigree as the man who came out of Adam's ribs in the Garden of Eden. Man was not made to be a cringing, crawling being, he was made to be a captain of his own ship, a master of his own destiny, and as he selects that much out of life he gets; nothing more."

He praised Prime Minister King again as a great statesman, contrasted him to a thief, and said both created their own lives.

"Is [former British Prime Minister] David Lloyd George a man? Is Mackenzie King a man? Answer that! Is Hitler a man? Answer that! Is Mussolini a man? Answer that! Are you a man? Answer that! Then ask yourself why these other men are different to you. God made no angels to inhabit this earth, God made no superior creature in man to inhabit this earth."

All men were created equal. All men (and presumably, although never stated, all women) remained equal in their essence. Each possesses a soul and a mind, shaped like God's. "And when any man in the image of God goes below the level he is not only reducing God in him, he is humiliating the God in him."

He expanded on his celestial ranking, topped by God, followed by angels, and only a little lower than angels: man. (And probably women.) God and humans coexist; one could not exist without the other, he said. And God exists as the "universal intelligence" and humans as a "universal part" of the deity who created the universe. God's goal was for humans to be happy and joyful.

Garvey returned to his earlier argument, stating that an unhappy human could blame neither God nor the earth, but only himself. "We are not seeking to disturb anybody. Each and every one of you sitting before me and any man who will come after, let him be Moses, or Joshua, let him be Abraham, let him be Mussolini or Hitler; you have in you the potential power of each and every creature who has gone before and each and every creature who will come after in the garb of man."

I wonder what he thought of pre-apocalypse Adolf Hitler. At this point in their lives, there existed parallels. Twenty years before, both Hitler and Garvey were penniless, essentially homeless, wandering lost in a world that didn't care about them. Both believed themselves to be great leaders of their scattered people – Hitler of the Germans, Garvey of the African diaspora. Both held clear views on race, and the importance of unity. One God, One Aim, One Destiny, said the UNIA. Ein volk, ein reich, ein Führer (one people, one empire, one leader), said the National Socialist party.

Both Hitler and Garvey came from places on the edges of their worlds and built themselves plinths of prominence. Hitler, born poor in rural Austria, now ruled Germany. Garvey, born poor in rural Jamaica, had titled himself President of Africa.

Both believed that individual human will was the determining factor in the world. And in 1937, Hitler was perhaps the most loved man on Earth, the champion of his adoring race, and the man leading his people into a glorious future. Garvey was not alone in praising Hitler.

Garvey had similar ambitions, but instead of speaking from his presidential palace in Africa, spoke to a small audience in Halifax, Nova Scotia.

You can be James Wolfe at the Plains of Abraham, he told them, or Abraham Lincoln signing the Emancipation Proclamation. You can be Prime Minister King, you can be Stalin, you can be Hitler. "You can play if you select that which is your function in life. There is no king without the thought of being a king, there is no sovereign or dictator without the thought in that direction. As man thinketh, so he is."

He described unfettered people, moving freely from obstacles in a society, rising to what they think they deserve. Humans think of empire, and then comes the empire. He looked down from the lectern to his audience. What did he read in their faces? What thoughts percolated behind their eyes?

"What are you thinking sitting down there? What are you thinking in Halifax? Everybody knows what you are thinking. You are thinking just of that humble position you occupy and that will be your position so long as you think fit. No man goes higher than his thoughts; as he thinks so shall he live and so shall he die. I am here only on my thoughts, not on my feet. I am here only on my thoughts and so are you."

He asked them to think about his words, to explore his ideas, long after he had physically left them. He hoped it would be worth the thirty-five cents they had paid to hear him talk. He returned then to his main theme, that humans determine their fate. "No intelligent man suffers," he said.

And surely a few intelligent men and women listening thought, What about Job? What about Moses? What about Jesus? What about us?

"You will say that is not a wise statement because you know educated people around here who still suffer," he said, perhaps reading their mood. "It is the duty of man to make his knowledge so complete in life as to make it impossible for any other man to take advantage of him."

A big task. He praised his audience for coming

out to learn tonight. "The man who knows walks the world a colossal success."

Those who don't know the world beg in it. "Man has made himself a fool," he said. "We have so many fools in the world and those are the people the others feed on."

I imagine a modern person might describe this as victim blaming. Garvey stormed onward.

"Your misfortune is the result of your lazy mentality. God did not bless the lazy servant, he blessed the intelligent servant who used his talent and multiplied," he lectured. "He cursed and drove away the lazy one."

A bitter Garvey hammered on, telling the people of Halifax that those who blamed the system earned no reward but death. "Halifax came out of the rocks and wilderness, Canada came out of the wilds of nature, London came out of the overflooded Thames and Paris out of the overflooded Seine," he continued.

"What I have to tell you could not be told in one hour, because of the peculiarity of your community. Ignorance will always make the attempt to hold back intelligence, but intelligence will always ride over ignorance and find its goal." But most people are too lazy to think, and therefore sink in ignorance, he argued. Men earn money to buy food to feed their stomachs, but spend little feeding their minds. "The men who eat up everything they lay their hands on go to their graves unwept, unsung, unhonoured."

Instead, honoured are the scientists, the thinkers, those who use intelligence, not force. The only difference between flourishing success and faltering failure is effort. Clear your thoughts, focus your will, and let your mind drive your body, he said.

"Whom did the white man ask for a job to lay the foundation of the city and the nation? He selected his own job to do his own building. He has built his own ships, air fleet, shaft, and goes down into the bosom of the earth and he goes up to the highest of the sky and he carries his commerce from one point to the next not with angels at the helm, but himself charting God's ocean," he thundered, bringing his great storm to its height.

"The race waits on you. It will never be greater than you make it and think of it. You haven't laid the foundation of your commercial system, your political system, yet you mimic the white man and say you are unemployed. This is nothing scarcely for him to do."

The white man has built this lovely city, he said, and now black people ask for a job. "You just follow him saying you are tired and you haven't laid a brick; you haven't sent one ship a thousand times across the ocean," he said. "When we tried, the Negro himself destroyed the project."

Acrimony coats these words. He quoted Booker T. Washington, saying his people were crabs in a basket, always pulling each other down. He grumbled that people only paid thirty-five cents a ticket to see him, when, he imagined, they'd have paid two dollars to hear a white man talk. "Any business man would decide that a people who wouldn't pay thirty-five cents to be enlightened have no attraction for him to waste his time upon."

I imagine there was a lot of uncomfortable shifting by now. These people had paid the entrance fee he asked for, and now were being insulted for not paying more.

"I cannot do anything for you in Halifax until you have made up your minds to do something for yourself. No man is completely helped from without, he is helped from within," he ended. "What are you going to give?"

And with that, the Black Moses left his people to turn back the Red Sea on their own.

★ ★ ★

Returning to London after his trip to Nova Scotia, Garvey opened his door and found not a warm family, but an empty house and a note explaining their absence. His second wife, Amy Jacques, had taken their sick son Marcus to the Caribbean in the hopes the sunshine would heal him.

He wrote to his sons, telling them he would not be able to join them in Jamaica. He signed it "Dad." The boys and the man kept up a heartbreaking correspondence, with Dad inquiring after their studies and sending gifts, while the boys wrote about what they learned at school.

As the Second World War slowly started across Europe, travelling across the Atlantic became more dangerous. Garvey could not sail to his family. He could not sail to Africa. He was stuck in London, the old capital of the white world.

"The collapse of the [UNIA] empire was sudden and tragic," reported the *New York Amsterdam News*. "With Garvey's exile he became a black Trotsky to the Negro masses. A sincere few tried to carry the UNIA along. [But] the old fire that could only be instilled by Garvey himself was lacking."

The military rise of Germany turned talk away

from things like black nationalism to more pressing threats: Hitler's panzers, U-boats, and Luftwaffe.

A leader with no followers, Garvey spent the last year of his life alone and lonely in London. His ex-wife, Amy Ashwood, chanced upon him one day in late 1939. She pitied the broken man. The bitterness over their divorce dissolved. She walked over and said hello and invited him to a nearby café to have a cup of tea together.

"I felt for a while the dynamic quality of Marcus," she later wrote. "Those little black eyes were still twinkling, but on this occasion filled with tears. There we were, our special version of 'Napoleon and Josephine,' and I remember hearing Marcus utter in a low calm voice, lines of moving beauty and truth:

The golden glory of love's light
Has never dawned on my way
My path has always led through night
To some deserted byway
But though life's greatest joy I miss,
There lies a greater strength than this
I have been worthy of it.

The two people, gathered again as a couple that had once faced a bright future arm in arm, walked quietly through the streets. Garvey stooped over his walking stick, the oldest fifty-two-year-old in England.

Later, with his former wife watching, he mounted his stepladder once more, and found the strength to straighten his drooping shoulders. The crowd jeered the comic figure. "He could no longer carry his listeners; even hecklers got the better of him. The Marcus I was listening to was no longer the 'Tiger,' the 'Black Moses,'" Ashwood wrote. "Tears were running from my eyes and I could stay in that place no longer. The old fire had gone."

As the winter of 1940 darkened, Hitler's white armies seized control of the world and vowed to kill off the weaker races.

Garvey's body failed him. He suffered a stroke and became paralyzed on his right side. His right hand was his writing hand. He could write no more. He could speak no more.

His family in Jamaica could not come to his side as he died. Amy Jacques took a photo of his healthy two boys and mailed it to him. He sobbed. He kept the photo under his pillow.

The remnant UNIA frantically raised funds from its diminished membership to help the Black Moses, and Garvey sent the money straight on to his family.

★ ★ ★

In May 1940, Marcus Garvey opened his morning newspaper and learned he was dead.

"Marcus Garvey Dies in London," wrote George Padmore in the *Chicago Defender*. The obituary spread across the world, and so Garvey got to see how the world would remember him. Many dumped hatred on his corpse, painting him as a fool and a failure. UNIA halls held respectful memorials.

But nothing funny lived in this moment, no "rumours of my death have been greatly exaggerated." He had already once risen from the apparent dead, when the assassin's bullet failed to kill him, but this second resurrection was unwitnessed. No Mary came to his tomb to weep until the gardener told her the good news.

Stung into silence, the shell-shocked warrior put down his worn-out tools for the last time. His will, so strong, so powerful, broke. Like France's Maginot Line, he was undone by an attack from above. As racist Nazi armies stormed across Europe and the entire world ignited, Marcus Garvey died alone in London on June 10, 1940.

His family had already buried him at a private service in Kingston. The Black Moses had climbed the mountain, had seen the Promised Land, and descended from his stepladder to find his people circling a golden calf.

Amy Ashwood, haunted by her last meeting with the man who once meant so much to her, dreamed of him after he died. Her husband came to her in the back of her home, and she saw him climb a great scaffolding, from which workers built an amazing ship.

"Build for Africa," he cried to her. "Work for Africa."

* * *

Garvey's dream of Africa for Africans came true. On the day he died, Liberia alone stood as a free country in Africa. European countries claimed colonial rule over every other African nation, including Italian-held Ethiopia.

Today, all of the more than fifty African countries are run by Africans. Africa is indeed for the Africans.

Garvey never lived to see what, at his birth, would have seemed impossible: colonial Europe withdrawing from Africa like a tide ebbing, followed by a wave of liberty breaking over the mother land. He never saw fifty-three free countries mapping their own lands, charting their own courses. Garvey learned of the genesis, encouraged the exodus, but did not hear the new testament. He also never saw lionized freedom fighters like Robert Mugabe storm the gates of the Promised Land and turn it into a hell.

In the Bible, Moses was succeeded by Joshua. Joshua led the Israelites into the Promised Land. Six years after the Black Moses died, his Joshua was born in Jamaica. But before we enter the Redemption Land with Bob Marley, we need to figure out where Garvey went wrong. And to do that, we must travel back in time to the invention of racism.

Song 15:
The Jericho Effect

The psychologist George Tamarin conducted an interesting moral study on children. He told them a short historical tale and asked them to judge the people in it. The tale happened in a Chinese kingdom three thousand years ago. General Lin is poised to take an enemy city and gives these commands to his troops:

General Lin said to the people, "Shout, for our god has given you the city. The city and all that is within it shall be devoted to the lord for destruction. But all the silver and gold, the vessels of bronze and iron, those are sacred to the lord; they shall go into the treasury of the lord."

Then they utterly destroyed all in the city, killing all the men and women, young and old, oxen, sheep, and donkeys, by stabbing and cutting them with swords. They then burned the entire city to the ground, thus killing anyone they'd missed with the swords. But they saved the silver and gold, and those vessels of bronze and iron – they put them in the treasury of the house of the lord.

Tamarin's question to the children – and mine to you – is: Do you think General Lin and his warriors acted morally?

The kids saw this clearly: 75 per cent of them flatly rejected General Lin's actions as immoral. Killing every single person in a city and then burning the whole thing to the ground is wrong.

Here comes the twist. Tamarin asked a different group of children the same question, but replaced "General Lin" with "Joshua" and told the above historical tale as it really is – it's the Old Testament's Book of Joshua and the city is Jericho, home of faulty wall engineers.

When asked about the morality of Joshua, 72 per cent of children voted he had acted morally – a complete reversal from their peers' take on General Lin. Yet the actions under examination were identical.

If the story hadn't changed, what had? Both groups of children were raised in religious (Jewish) schools and had been raised to see the Old Testament stories not through a neutral lens, but through the lens of them being on one team (the Jews) and opposed to the other (the people of Jericho).

An alien visiting us from Kepler-186f, an Earth-like planet circling a star five hundred light years from our Sun in the Cygnus constellation, would have no such confusion. If we're judging pure morality, changing the names of the actors makes no difference. General Lin and Joshua are equally reprehensible or admirable, our alien would decide.

But we're not from Kepler-186f. We're from

Earth. The Jericho Effect leads us to see the world through our own minds, to see ourselves as superior creatures, to by default assume we ourselves have acted morally.

★ ★ ★

J.S. Frideres, director of the indigenous studies department at the University of Calgary, provides a useful definition of racism. It comes from the online *Canadian Encyclopedia*:

"Racism is an ideology that claims the human species can be divided into discrete biological groupings that determine the behaviour, economic, and political success of individuals within that group.

"This belief views races as natural and fixed subdivisions of humans, each with its distinct and variable cultural characteristics and capacity for developing civilizations. Thus, the biological factors can be used to explain the social and cultural variations of humans."

Beautifully simple. Something Marcus Garvey could have written himself. Or his friend, Ku Klux Klan Imperial Wizard Edward Young Clarke. But, of course, racism lasts in that ideal state for 0.001 seconds before being corrupted by the Jericho Effect. Like those schoolchildren, humans accepting this theory tend to think their race is better than the rest.

George Frederickson, history professor at Stanford University and author of *Racism: A Short History*, observes that racism quickly turns into oppression, with the dominant group excluding or eliminating the weaker group on the basis of those "hereditary and unalterable" differences between those proposed racial groups.

Humans have probably forever stigmatized "others" as less valuable than themselves. Tel Aviv University professor Benjamin Isaac pursues the idea's roots back to Classical Antiquity and the way Greeks and Persians saw each other as being of different tribes (he calls it proto-racism). They believed in "environmental determinism, the belief in the heritability of acquired characteristics and the belief in the importance of lineage," he finds.

But Frederickson rejects that idea. He says the Greeks and Persians distinguished between civilized and barbarous, but didn't see barbarity as hereditary and unalterable. You could learn better and rise in life. This becomes clearly true when those cultures became Christian and Muslim, both religions that actively seek to convert people to their elevated status. They could discriminate against Jewish people, but as of the thirteenth century did so as though Jews were people with wrong ideas, not wrong blood.

The word "race" in the sense of people of common descent first turns up in the 1560s as a French word describing a person's tribe or family. The *Oxford English Dictionary* says race's meaning of "one of the great divisions of mankind based on physical peculiarities" was first used in 1774.

Isaac argues the proto-racism leeched a ride along the centuries of European thought before surfacing again in the Middle Ages.

Racism took its first semi-scientific steps toward modernity when people started seeing race as something like species, and focusing the oppression on Jewish people. In 1215, European Christianity officially declared that Jews and Muslims must be marked out from other citizens by dressing differently. In 1218, England's rulers forced Jews to wear badges on their chests. By 1290, England's rulers took a hard turn and forced Jews out of the country. The Crusades led to many massacres of Jews and Muslims (and Christians) across Europe.

People at this time had a lot of dumb ideas that barely require rejection today. For example, Christian Europeans believed Jewish men menstruated like women and that Jewish bodies stank differently than other bodies. As early as 1150, European Christians started thinking that Jews crucified Christian children in evil rituals. In 1215, Christian leaders made transubstantiation (the belief that communion wine and wafers physically become the blood and flesh of Christ) an article of faith and soon people accused Jews of stealing the host and torturing the bread to re-enact the killing of Jesus. Christians started to see this as deliberate unbelief – not that Jews didn't know about Christ, but that they knew and actively opposed.

And then Black Death raped Europe.

⋆ ⋆ ⋆

When plague slaughtered millions of people across Europe in an invisible terror, some people – knowing nothing of germs – came to think Jews were poisoning the water to murder them. In the chaos of that great dying, when about one in two Europeans experienced a monstrous death, cultural prejudices against Jews hardened into something angrier, more vengeful.

Thousands of Jewish people who survived the plague were massacred or driven out of Christendom. More and more people started thinking the Jews couldn't be saved. That the fault was not in their ideas, but in their blood.

★ ★ ★

The Jericho Effect revealed itself in *De Proprietatibus Rerum* (*On The Properties of Things*), an "encyclopedia" of wild ideas collected by Bartholomew the Englishman sometime in the 1200s. He said cold climates produce white people, hot ones black people. Bartholomew was white. Guess which colour he thought was better? White. White skin, he said, is a visible marker of inner courage. Black skin, he lectured, showed "cowards of heart."

In the 1300s, *Cursor Mundi* (or *Runner of the World*, a historical and religious poem) recalls a magical day when biblical King David met four Saracens. David, a white guy in this telling, feels pity for the nameless Saracens, who are black guys. So he invites them to kiss Moses's rod. And behold: "Their skin became as white as milk and they had the hue of noble blood."

But Frederickson argues this is not part of the anti-black racism we're talking about in *Redemption Songs*. Before the 1400s, Europeans had little or no contact with Africans living south of the Saharan desert. Europeans imagined Africans much as they did the sea beasts drawn on oceanic maps. Strange, exotic, at turns wonderful and at turns horrifying.

In fact, Negrophilia swept across Europe in the Middle Ages. Christian Europeans fought repeatedly with Islam, and saw the rival religion as an existential threat. Christian Europe looked over the Islamic world and saw black Africa on the other side. An amazing legend materialized: that of Prester John, a black Christian king who ruled a vast, wealthy, and powerful empire on the far side of the caliphate.

Europeans dreamed and expected Prester John to attack Islam from the south, while Christian Europe invaded from the north. The pincer assault would crush Islam and give Christianity the final triumph.

Many identified Prester John as the black king of Ethiopia. None imagined his black skin showed an innate condition of inferiority. White Europe turned to black Africa for the ultimate alliance that would win the world for Christianity.

Balthasar, one of the three kings who brought gold, frankincense, and myrrh to baby Jesus, turned black in Christian art and became the ancestor of Prester John. The once-white Saint Maurice turned black, too, especially in German lands. Saint Gregory the Moor, a black man, grew in popularity. Statues and paintings of the Black Madonna showed Mary and Jesus with dark skin.

Many white Europeans saw Africa as a land of purer Christians.

* * *

The roots of European anti-black racism grew in Spain in the 1400s and 1500s. Christians and Muslims lived together for a time, in some peace. Muslims brought the idea that black people descended from Ham, the cursed son of Noah, and were thus lesser humans. Slaves were common, and Muslims held white and black slaves. But if a Christian saw a white person with a powerful Muslim, she could only guess the white person was a slave; if she saw a black person, she knew they were a slave.

And so people started associating skin colour with slavery. It was a badge you could not take off.

Christians felt uneasy about enslaving Christians, but fine with enslaving heathens. And enslave them they did, regardless of skin colour. But Christianity's conquest of Europe reduced the pool of white slaves. Serbians and Russians were officially recognized as Christians in 1356 and 1589, respectively. The Slavs – the very people whose name gives us the word slave – also became Christians, and so off limits as potential slaves.

White people who once would have been slaves were instead ransomed back to liberty, or exchanged for other prisoners. But tribal Africans were generally not Christians, and so taking them as slaves grew more appealing. As Europe ran out of white slaves, it turned to Africa.

Portuguese merchants began catching Africans and enslaving them.

★ ★ ★

In 1578, George Best wrote a popular account of Martin Frobisher's explorations in what is now Canada's far north. He loved colonial adventuring, but worried that if the environment shaped how people looked, then white Europeans would turn black under certain circumstances. (Of course we now know that is true, but that it takes thousands of years and certain conditions of evolution.)

To alleviate his fears of turning black on his travels, Best promoted a belief that colour and racial type were fixed. Whiteness and blackness were hereditary, unalterable conditions. This idea hung out with the thought black people were Ham's children and formed a coalition that solidified European belief that black people were born to be slaves. Born to be inferior. Maybe not even human.

★ ★ ★

In the 1600s, plantation owners in the Americas had to choose their source of labour. White people could be taken as indentured servants, but they were more expensive than slaves. And they were generally Christians. First Nations people were the nearest and cheapest source of heathen slaves, but the catastrophic introduction of Old World diseases killed millions of indigenous people. They also had home field advantage and could escape back to their tribes.

Africans, already long-exposed to many of the same diseases as Europeans, adapted better and survived longer in the new world. It was harder for them to escape, too, as they spoke no local languages and at first had no idea where they were. So Africans became the dominant group of slaves.

Black slaves and indentured white servants had a lot in common, and poor black and white humans sometimes worked together to better their situation.

In 1676, Virginian Nathaniel Bacon organized an uprising of hundreds of farmers, servants, and slaves – black and white – against the Virginia Tidewater planters. The Englishman's ragtag army sacked Jamestown and the governor fled. Bacon's troops held Jamestown for eight months before being defeated. After the defeat, the Tidewater planters split the army's potential recruits apart. They offered a slightly better life for white people, and a worse one for black people. (Think back to our discussion of Shelburne and Birchtown in Songs 4 and 5.)

Laws were drawn up to protect the slave-owners' human property. Some were already on the books. In Maryland in 1664, the legislature declared that slave status passed through the mother, so any child born to an enslaved woman was also a slave, and the property of the slave-owner. The law doesn't describe this in racial terms – it's interested in property. But that property was black.

When Americans declared all men are created equal a century later, the authors of the Declaration of Independence understood that it didn't apply to men (or women) who were black. Thomas Jefferson, the man who wrote the declaration, called slavery "moral depravity" and a "hideous blot." He argued the new country should free some slaves and tried to pass a Virginia law to emancipate young enslaved Africans.

He had plenty of opportunity to study black people, as he owned 175 Africans and forced them to live as slaves.

Another victim of the Jericho Effect, Jefferson concluded that white people are just naturally more beautiful than black people. "Is [race] not the foundation of a greater or less share of beauty in the two races?" he asked in the 1780s. "The circumstance of superior beauty is thought worthy attention in the propagation of our horses, dogs and other domestic animals. Why not in that of man?"

His contemporary, the British surgeon Charles White, agreed. Both men observed how it was interesting that only white women could blush. Perhaps black women had no shame? White also asked, "where, except on the bosom of the European woman, [shall we find] two such plump and snowy white hemispheres, tipt with vermillion?"

Jefferson did think emancipation would come one day – he described slavery as like holding "a wolf by the ear, and we can neither hold him, nor safely let him go." Some of those wolves were his own biological children, but he used that ever-flexible human mind to see his own genetic progeny as genetically inferior to himself.

The Stanford Prison Experiment had become law: the children of guards were guards, and the children of prisoners were prisoners. Eventually, people forgot how the great division started.

★ ★ ★

Having your whole society fundamentally divided between free and slave creates deep instability. In the earlier periods of European slavery, the slaves were heathens or barbarians and thus had a way out. They could theoretically convert. You could always capture more.

But the Atlantic slave trade relied on each generation of slaves producing the next. The dominant group needed a story to explain why this was permanent and unchanging. People felt uneasy and so turned to the old idea of race once again, but now discussed in scientific terms.

It was clearly inhumane to grab people from their homes, chain them, stuff them into slaves ships like stacked firewood, and force them to work eighteen-hour days year-round for the rest of their lives. So – perhaps the slaves weren't humans?

★ ★ ★

In the next centuries, Europeans were suddenly pushing exploration into Africa, Asia, and the Americas like never before. As Europeans encountered humans living radically different lives all over the world, they started to solidify the idea of racism, and the Jericho Effect led them to believe their racial group (white) was the best.

This was a world dominated (from a European perspective) by religion: there were Christians and heathens. Of course post-Reformation, that "Christian" category splintered into smaller and smaller groups of pure people battling heretic Christians.

As the Industrial Revolution revealed the overwhelming power of science over religion, racism ideas drifted away from divine definitions and toward scientific arguments. But ditching the Bible's views on the topic meant ditching the belief that all humans were God's children descended from Adam and Eve, and therefore all were related.

European explorers had long reported half-human beasts in the wilds of the world. In 1625, British explorer Andrew Batell found in Angola a humanoid monster covered in fur, except for his face and hands, who stood like a man but "with the stature of a giant."

Europeans had for some time thought Africans were black because they lived under hotter suns. Then they met people in today's Brazil and saw they had tawny skin in the same climate. So why was African skin black? Maybe it was the sign of the biblical curse placed on Ham. Maybe it was God's way as marking them as slaves.

But Christianity's great call to freedom, and the deep belief that all humans actually descended from Adam and Eve, created a strong barrier in the European mind against fully embracing the ideology of racism.

★ ★ ★

In 1856, French adventurer Paul Du Chaillu followed Mbondemo guides into the woods of Gabon, West Africa, and they showed him a massive animal. "The forearms bulged with the promise of strength, its neck a massive pillar of solid muscle. The animal must have weighed nearly 400 pounds," he later wrote.

His guides shot it dead and roasted it up into a delicious meal. Du Chaillu declined to eat the animal, but did start collecting skins from the creatures. He brought parts of twenty-one such animals to London in 1861 and showed it to the public. Behold: the gorilla. (Monte Reel tells the whole fascinating story in *Between Man and Beast*.)

Could this be a missing link between humans and the rest of the animal kingdom? Chailu and many European thinkers detected a suspicious similarity between the gorilla (long thought to be a mythical beast) and the black guys who showed it to him.

When Charles Darwin published his explosive *On the Origin of Species* in 1859, racism seemed to have found solid scientific grounds. If animals evolved into different species, and the fittest species rose to the top, wasn't it logical that humans were in fact different species, marked by race, and that the fittest naturally rose to the top? And who was presently at the top? White people.

★ ★ ★

Darwin imagined a human tribe growing and expanding across the land not as explorers, but more like a son building a house on the edge of his parents' property. His daughter does the same thing, and over time your tribe spreads across the continent. War and distance would separate the ancestral grandmothers from their descendant grandsons.

"The hordes would thus be exposed to slightly different conditions and habits of life, and would sooner or later come to differ in some small degree," he wrote in *The Descent of Man and Selection in Relation to Sex*.

Much of it would be random mutations changing features to no advantage, but merely as a process of genetic drift. Other changes would be selected by climate. Darwin also thought sexual selection played a peacock role. If women decided dark skin was more attractive and selected dark-skinned men to mate with, the whole tribe would gradually get darker. "Thus the differences between the tribes, at first very slight, would gradually and inevitably be more or less increased," Darwin wrote.

★ ★ ★

When Charles Darwin sailed the world on the *Beagle*, he flipped through an encyclopedia that helpfully divided humankind into fifteen separate species, each with a different root. He met humans in Tierra del Fuego and found one "can hardly make oneself believe that they are fellow creatures."

Many modern Westerners experience culture shock when visiting China, or Turkey, or Egypt, but it's easy to see the other people are fellow creatures. But then we've never met someone who had never met someone outside of their tribe. We've never met someone who lived as a forager on an island off the coast of South America, steeped in an 11,000-year-old culture utterly unconnected to ours. It's hard for us to imagine the experience felt on both sides as groups of humans contacted for the very first time.

"The civilized races of man will almost certainly exterminate, and replace, the savage races throughout the world," Darwin wrote in *The Descent of Man*. He didn't think this was a good thing – just inevitable.

He offered a brighter vision of the future:

"As man advances in civilization, and small tribes are united into larger communities, the simplest reason would tell each individual that he ought to extend his social instincts and sympathies to all the members of the same nation, though personally unknown to him. This point being once reached, there is only an artificial barrier to prevent his sympathies extending to the men of all nations and races.

"If, indeed, such men are separated from him by great differences in appearance or habits, experience unfortunately shews us how long it is, before we look at them as our fellow-creatures."

Most people ignored this part of Darwin's thinking and focused on the survival of the fittest. Up until then, Europeans understood their increasing dominance of the world as due to their technological advantages and divine guidance. But people started thinking maybe white people were innately fitter. Maybe black people were born prisoners.

Song 16:
Hitler Ruins Racism

In September 1906, New York's Bronx Zoo brought in a popular new animal to be exhibited in an iron monkey house. His name was Ota Benga, and he was an African. Specifically, he was from Congo. His appearance was promoted as your chance to see the Pygmy in the Zoo.

Benga was about twenty-three when he found himself exhibited in the Bronx Zoo. He fell into his misadventure two years before when he was captured and sold to Samuel Phillips Verner, a white American man who had travelled to Africa specifically to hunt Africans for display in the 1904 St. Louis World's Fair, a.k.a. the Louisiana Purchase Exhibition. One white person described Benga as a "dwarfy, black specimen of sad-eyed humanity."

Some of that sorrow no doubt came from King Leopold II. The Belgian ruler grew into a monster of the ancient Roman variety when he pacified Congo.

Congo had rubber plants, which was then a highly valuable crop in Europe. Leopold's militia attacked Benga's village and killed his wife and two children. Benga was out hunting at the time and returned to find his world utterly destroyed.

Few humans have explored the world's cultures quite like Benga did, and when he arrived to be displayed at the Louisiana Purchase Exhibition, he charmed the Americans. He showed them his sharp teeth, filed to a point as was his cultural custom, and earned money posing for photographs. One newspaper imagined he was a genuine "African cannibal."

Benga and the other Africans he was displayed with noticed the American Indian war displays were popular, so they invented war displays of their own to draw crowds. Verner received a Gold Medal in Anthropology at the end of the exhibition.

Benga found lodging as a display in the American Museum of Natural History, where visitors watched him tend a fake campfire and feed fake meat to a fake child.

In 1906, Verner arranged for Benga to move into the Bronx Zoo with an orangutan named Dohong. Both lived in the Monkey House. Neither was a monkey. Benga, like all humans, was a type of ape, as was Dohong.

Benga shot a bow and arrow and wandered the woods of his fake wilderness.

James H. Gordon, a black American, saw the whole thing as a disgrace. "Our race, we think, is depressed enough without exhibiting one of us with the apes. We think we are worthy of being considered human beings with souls," he protested. Gordon, a clergyman, argued that it was anti-Christian, too, as God had created all humans equally and all humans could be saved by God's grace.

The New York Times dismissed his concerns. "It is absurd to make moan over the imagined humiliation and degradation Benga is suffering," it editorialized. "The pygmies are very low in the human scale."

The newspaper thought it would be ridiculous to put him in a school instead of a cage, as he could not possibly benefit from an education. "The idea that men are all much alike except as they have had or lacked opportunities for getting an education out of books is now far out of date."

Around Christmas 1906, Benga was released from the zoo. Gordon arranged for the twenty-three-year-old to live in an orphanage. He later moved to Virginia. He started dressing like an American and trying to conceal his origins. But he apparently disliked his new life and started organizing a return to Africa.

The Great War broke out in 1914, and suddenly sailing home became impossible. In 1916, Benga chipped the caps off to reveal his sharpened teeth. He built a ceremonial fire. He shot himself in the heart and died.

* * *

George Frederickson argues that the decline of Christianity removed an important barrier against the ideology of racism. Once white people no longer believed all humans descended from Adam by the hand of God, they could start to see some humans as innately lesser than others. The two groups that suffered the worst during peak racism were black people and

Jewish people.

In Racism: A Short History, Frederickson argues that the crucial difference was when North American governments explicitly stated as fact the core idea of racism: that there are permanent and unbridgeable differences between human races. And the Jericho Effect meant that the white people making and internalizing these ideas unquestioningly saw themselves as superior.

The Western ideas of racial purity blossomed in the dawn of the twentieth century. But racism has a fatal flaw. As Thomas Jefferson showed, white men can have sex with black women and produce babies who prove racism is false. The baby is neither black nor white, or both black and white. The ideology of racism could not survive such a challenge, so extreme penalties were placed on anyone who would intimately cross the colour line. Sex between the races had to be stopped to make a plausible case for the ideology of racism.

To further maintain the ideology of racial superiority, black people weren't permitted to vote or hold high office. Frederickson finds this enforced ideology reaches its fullest expression against black people in the Jim Crow U.S. south, in South Africa, and against Jewish people in Nazi Germany.

Just as Communists would later try to force their ideology on reality, so too did the believers of the ideology of racism seek to force their ideas on reality. They built the prisons around the people they believed to be natural prisoners.

★ ★ ★

Frederickson thinks humiliation is at the root of much of the twentieth century's worst racism. He thinks Jim Crow America, apartheid South Africa, and Holocaust Germany were revenge for humiliation.

Many southern black Americans had escaped slavery and fought on the side of the victorious North in the recent U.S. Civil War. The white dream of a "free" South was crushed in large part by African-Americans. Many of the defeated white Americans grew bitter seeds of hatred in their hearts. If only the black people hadn't fought against them, they would have won.

In South Africa, the Afrikaners thought they had been defeated by the British in the Boer War of 1899-1902 because most black Africans fought with the British. If only the Africans hadn't fought against them, they would have won.

In 1918, many defeated Germans blamed the Jews for stabbing them in the back. People like Adolf Hitler, a grunt soldier in the First World War, believed that the German army was on the cusp of victory in 1918 when international Jewry (and specifically German Jews) sold their victory for personal profit. The true reasons for how it seemed to a grunt that Germany was on the edge of victory when in fact it was crashing into defeat are beyond the scope of this book. Download the free podcast *Hardcore History: Blueprint for Armageddon* for a deeper understanding. If only the Jews hadn't turned against them, they would have won.

In each case, the poisonous broth of defeat, humiliation, and scapegoating turned rancid under the ideology of racism.

★ ★ ★

Today's visitors to Auschwitz-Birkenau in Poland are routinely startled to find a section of the murder camp called "Canada."

When the German soldiers corralled humans who were Jewish into ghettos across Europe, they needed a way to convince them to pack their valuables and get on a train to a new location. The Germans told the Jews they were going to Canada. The poorest people of Europe saw a vision of a new life in that great, wealthy country famous for its freedom, and so boarded the trains.

Packed in tightly on the cattle cars, the Jewish people probably knew something was wrong when the trains travelled east, not west. As the trains pulled into the sprawling Birkenau camp, Nazi guards told the people to stack their possessions in a pile by the train.

The women, children, and weak then immediately proceeded along a short walk to the gas chamber and crematorium. The men were forced into slave labour until they worked themselves to death.

Their goods – suitcases full of nice dresses, hats, glasses, heirlooms – went to Canada. This Canada was a warehouse where the guards stored the prisoners' possessions for processing. It was an inside joke: the guards knew Canada as a land of great riches and so nicknamed their stolen wealth after it.

Most of the goods were sorted and sent back to the central treasury in Berlin. Often, trains full of those belongings would chug west past trains full of thousands of victims heading east to Canada. Some lucky Jews worked in Canada. "Working in Canada saved my life because we had food, we got water. And that was the best working unit for life because we were not beaten," remembered inmate Libusa Breder.

In Canada, you could also grow out your hair to reclaim a bit of your humanity. Sometimes you found extra food in the suitcases and snuck a snack. Sometimes guards even violated the fundamental Nazi rules against sex between Jews and Gentiles by striking up relationships with the prisoners.

Helena Citronova arrived at Canada from Slovakia. She caught the eye of an SS guard named Frank Wunsch. "When he came into the barracks where I was working, he threw me a note. I destroyed it right there and then, but I did see the word 'love' – 'I fell in love with you,'" she said after the war. "I thought I'd rather be dead than be involved with an SS man. For a long time afterwards, there was just hatred. I couldn't even look at him."

But then her sister and her sister's children arrived inside the barbed wire. Citronova turned to the love-struck Nazi for help. He raced to the trains and pulled her sister out of the line to the gas chambers by saying she worked for him in Canada. He saved her life. He didn't help her children.

* * *

In 1939, 907 Jewish refugees sailed across the Atlantic Ocean with their bags packed for Canada. The *St. Louis* was rejected from landing in Cuba, America, and then Halifax. George Wrong, a history professor who actually turned out to be right, led a group of ministers and professors pressing Prime Minister William Lyon Mackenzie King to accept the refugees. The prime minister declined. Halifax turned the ship away and it was forced to return to Europe.

They were rejected on the ground of racism. Canada didn't want too many Jews. Many Nova Scotians sighed with relief.

★ ★ ★

Adolf Hitler believed fundamentally in the truth of the ideology of racism. We're talking about the Austrian Adolf, not the Indian Adolf.

So many people agreed with Hitler that he was voted into control of one of the largest, most advanced, most powerful countries in the world. With the tools of a fully modernized, industrialized, civilized country in his hands, he put racism into practice.

People like the Jews and Gypsies were officially declared to be separate, lower, and malevolent races of sub-humans. Hitler offered a vision of the Jew that could stand for the fullest expression of the urgency of the racist global agenda, the white man's burden to tame the wild world:

"With satanic joy in his face, the black-haired Jewish youth lurks in wait for the unsuspecting girl whom he defiles with his blood, thus stealing her from her people. With every means he seeks to destroy the racial foundations of the people he has set out to subjugate. Just as he himself systematically ruins women, he does not shrink from pulling down the blood barriers for others, even on a large scale.

"It was and it is Jews who bring the Negroes into the Rhineland, always with the same secret thought and clear aim of ruining the hated white race by the necessarily resulting bastardization, throwing it down from its cultural and political height, and himself rising to be its master."

Hitler reveals the absolute core of the ideology of racism, and shows how weak its foundations. The University of Berkeley defines species this way: "The biological species concept defines a species as members of populations that actually or potentially interbred in nature." By definition, if two animals can breed, they are of the same species. So the clearest expression of the ideology of racism in fact shows the entire theory is a sham. If you have to prevent people from making children, those people are by definition the same species.

Hitler's deepest fears and extensive laws against breeding demonstrated conclusively that there is only one human species. Frederickson describes World War Two as "the climax and turning point in the history of racism in the twentieth century."

People learned about the death camps after the war. They saw what racism really was. "The resulting shock and mortification did more to discredit racism … than had any previous historical event," Frederickson writes.

The ignoble regime of white supremacy in South Africa and the shameful anti-black Jim Crow era in America further revealed the ideology's flaws. Nelson Mandela and Martin Luther King Jr. presented final, personal testimony against the theory that black people were dumb animals.

In 1950, the world's leading geneticists and physical anthropologists studied the scientific underpinnings of the ideology of racism. The DNA information produced no evidence that human groups varied in "their innate capacity for intellectual and emotional development" and "no reliable evidence that disadvantageous effects are produced" by people of different colours having children.

If losing the Christian belief in Adam and Eve as divinely created progenitors of all humanity cracked open the vial of poison we call racism, we can turn to the scientific understanding of Adam and Eve as the antidote. As Marcus Garvey told us in Song 7, we must look not to Eden, but Ethiopia.

But first we have to figure out if Bob Marley was black or white.

Song 17:
Does it matter if you're black or white?

In June 2015, the head of the NAACP in Spokane, Washington, spoke to reporter Jeff Humphrey about racist mail she'd been receiving. She described it as a hate crime against her as a black woman. When she lived in North Idaho, she'd found a noose hanging in her front yard as her sons played. She'd had plenty of hate mail before, too, and other nooses. In fact, she said the Ku Klux Klan, Neo Nazis, and Aryan Nation were among the groups that had tormented her in North Idaho with at least eight documented hate crimes. "I would love to live in a world where hate crimes don't exist," she lamented.

The prominent civil rights activist had spent much of her life campaigning against anti-black racism and celebrating her black identity. She taught Africana Education at Eastern Washington University, and also taught African-American art, history, and culture, focusing on the black woman's struggle.

She had First Nations roots, too, and was born in a Montana tepee. Her family lived off the land for her early years, hunting with bow and arrow. She said even her own mother and stepfather were racist, punishing their darker children "by skin complexion" with a device she called a baboon whip.

Humphrey, the TV reporter, then posed a simple question. "Is that your dad?" he asked, holding a photo she'd posted online of her standing next to her father, a black man.

She hesitated and then answered yes.

"Are you African-American?" he asked.

"I don't understand the question," she replied, and then ripped off her microphone and ended the interview. She fled, leaving her keys and purse.

Her name was Rachel Dolezal.

A couple of days later her mother and father – both white – did a media tour denouncing their daughter as a faker and showing photos of her as a blonde, white child.

The "noose" turned out to be a rope, not a noose, and it had been left hanging in the yard by a previous occupant, a hunter, who strung a deer up for cleaning. The letters hadn't been franked, so they hadn't been mailed to her. One of the few keyholders must have placed them in the post office box. (Dolezal had a key.)

Her parents said Dolezal spent years shifting her identity from white to black, and cutting them out was part of that process. She dyed her blonde hair darker and curled it. She used tanning products to darken her skin.

A February 2015 pre-scandal profile of Dolezal

revealed the writer was surprised by her "unexpected green eyes" and "caramel skin complexion," but accepted her black identity. I mean, who wouldn't?

Post-scandal, Dolezal's black son, who turned out to be her adopted brother, denounced her as wearing blackface and said she had indeed used make-up to darken her face and hair products to give herself an Afro.

Dolezal called herself "trans-racial," and many people quickly tied her story to another one dominating the spring headlines: former Olympian Bruce Jenner's transgendering into Caitlyn Jenner.

Can you choose your racial identity? Can you decide if you're black or white inside – and then match that on the outside?

* * *

Bob Marley had to decide if he was black or white. His father, Captain Norval Sinclair Marley, was a white man from England. His mother, Cedella Booker, was a black woman from Jamaica. Marley was born with that twoness and had to decide which identity to embrace.

Few photos survive of Captain Marley. The most reproduced one depicts the British officer sitting on a horse. Born in Essex, England, he served in India before being transferred to colonial Jamaica. Tall and imposing, Marley patrolled the plantations of St. Ann (Marcus Garvey's birth town), befriending kids and offering polite greetings to the predominantly black population in his charge.

Marley, fifty, grew especially friendly with a nineteen-year-old gospel singer named Cedella Booker. The couple became intimate, and Booker became pregnant.

Marley asked his "Ciddy" to sing for him as they courted, and promised her marriage and a happy life. In the tense moments before they married in June 1944, the captain took his pregnant fiancée aside and told her he would soon leave for Kingston, and would never return. He did not ask her to come with him. He had brought news of their relationship to his white family, but they rejected the black pregnant woman entirely and threatened to disinherit the captain if he stayed involved.

The couple married anyway and had a son on February 6, 1945, whom they named Robert Nesta Marley. Marley entered a Jamaica that would have been depressingly familiar to the recently departed Marcus Garvey: poor, hungry bellies growling during a beef shortage, cold skin shivering through chilled nights of unlit fires because of a shortage of matches.

Norval Marley returned to work in Kingston.

Robert was raised by his mother and her family, especially his grandfather Omeriah. His grandfather saw the boy's name as a slave name – both the first name, Robert (he was named after Norval's brother), and the last name, Marley. While many a Jamaican believed white to be best, and brown better than black, Omeriah scorned such self-hatred and embraced his African ancestors.

After a few months, Norval took leave from his government job and spent a week with his infant son. In the coming years, he wrote the occasional letter, and received replies, but then he moved and sent no forwarding address. Financial support arrived sporadically.

Nesta, as his mother called her baby, grew up in a shack, always seeking a way to make sense of his black and white roots, his African and European DNA. He worked the fields with his mother, carrying water and messages between the workers, learning the agricultural trade.

The observing boy loved when the family gathered to sing songs, tell stories of Africa, and listen to a cousin's story of Prester John, the legendary lost black Christian king of Asia Minor. No white person, be they king, knight, or peasant, ever earned an audience with the dark monarch.

Others spoke of the great Haile Selassie, Emperor of Ethiopia, who had fought the Fascist Italian army in World War Two. By the time of Marley's birth, Selassie was re-enthroned in Addis Ababa.

Marley learned about Marcus Garvey, the great Jamaican prophet who foretold the coming of the black king. The boy hid behind his mother as another teller told of the blackheart man, a brute born and dying in darkness, wandering friendless and unfamilyed through the gutters, with hair tangled like dead snakes. Timothy White tells the story in *Catch a Fire* – and notes that the figure who so terrified Robert Marley was a Rastafarian.

Rastas dressed and acted like street people, or people suffering from untreated mental health crises, and invited that stigma upon themselves. Much like Jesus hanging out with prostitutes and tax collectors, Rastas scared people by favouring the downtrodden.

Nesta developed a reputation as a palm reader in a land of magical realism. He had an aura of the supernatural, like he was always half in this world and half in the spiritual realm.

⋆ ⋆ ⋆

Bob Marley grew up black, but his whiteness kept checking in. When he was five, a letter arrived at the family's small home. Captain Marley wanted to see his son. He decided his boy should be adopted by a Marley – specifically his brother's son – to open professional doors. The nephew was a successful businessman at Marley & Plant in Kingston.

Marley's St. Ann's family at first rejected the offer, afraid the boy would be broken permanently from them. The captain followed up with an offer to move his son to Kingston so he could go to the better schools there. His mother brooded over the offer. She doubted her ability to raise him properly. She decided, with the rest of the family, to send him to the capital.

Nesta sobbed at first because his mother would be separated from him, but took the country bus to the big city. It was the first time he'd been in a motor vehicle. It was also the first time he'd seen white people in big numbers.

At the bus station, a white man took his hand. Nesta shrieked and leapt for freedom, before the man settled him. "I'm your bloody father, Robert," Captain Marley said.

The father gathered his son, put him in a donkey cart, climbed into the driver's seat, and started the donkey on the bumpy journey home.

His mother heard nothing for a year, and finally worry overcame her. She travelled to Kingston and searched high and low for her son before she found him kicking a soccer ball down a Kingston street. He lived there with an elderly woman hired by Captain Marley to be his caretaker.

Ciddy brought her boy home.

Later, the captain married another woman. He aged poorly. Fatted, wobbly, and flat-footed, the once sprightly man who charmed children with small gifts had crashed into the end of his life. Ciddy confronted Marley – and his new wife – with the news that he was still married to her.

Bucked by a world he ill-fit, Marley barely seemed to have knowledge of anything, anymore. Ciddy sued him for bigamy. Nesta stole glimpses of his father at the court hearing.

The man had life rolling-pinned out of him, and he died flat and crushed in 1955. With him died Nesta's connection to the European DNA that gave him that slender nose and light skin.

"My father was a guy you know, from England. Him was like … like you can read it you know, it's one of dem slave stories: white guy get the black woman and breed her. He's a English guy, I tink. My mother? My mother African," Bob Marley said as an adult.

His white father was gone. He sought a black father to replace him.

* * *

Marley and his mother moved to a poor area of Kingston called Trench Town. The humming community sang the blues, and the sky bounced with jumbo speakers pulsating Fats Domino and Amos Millburn into the humid air.

It was a very black neighbourhood and Marley

stuck out as "that white boy."

A teenage romance ended because the black girl's family didn't want her mixing with a white man – Bob Marley. Many black people didn't trust him. Why was this white man living in black Trench Town?

Some saw him as brown – that third race category we saw in Marcus Garvey's story. Brown people, a.k.a. mulattos, suffered doubly. Many black Jamaicans distrusted and disliked them, and most whites scorned their supposed inferiors. Marley's identity was shaped profoundly by this double alienation.

He tried to reject either racial identity.

"Well, me don't dip on nobody's side. Me don't dip on the black man's side nor the white man's side. Me dip on God's side, the one who created me and cause me to come from black and white, who give me this talent," Marley said.

But no one gets to truly decide on their racial identity. It's a decision everyone else makes about you.

★ ★ ★

After the Kingston adventure, Bob Marley returned to rural Jamaica and traded the gift of palm reading for the gift of singing.

"How he do things and prophesy things, he is not just by himself. He have higher powers, even from when he is a little boy. The way I felt, the kind of vibes I get when Bob comes around ... It's too honorable. I always look upon him with great respect. There is something inside me telling me that he is not only a son, there is something greater in this man," his mother said.

Nesta attended school, but struggled to make

friends. A teacher at the school blamed his half-caste colour, which made the black kids fear he felt superior to them. And so they drove him out, and so he sought out teachers, and thrived on their attention.

He built guitars out of sardine tins and bamboo and accompanied his own whispered songs. His inner radiance eventually won the kids around and his popularity increased. He excelled at math.

When he was twelve, his family moved back to Kingston's Trench Town. The "trench" in question was the sewage ditch the town sat on. The town was built next to the old dump after the 1951 earthquake. The concrete houses clustered around the government yards of communal cooking areas and the water pump. There was no sewage system. It was very similar to Africville.

Trench Town housed the outcasts, including Rastas, tellable by their matted hair and the clouds of marijuana smoke.

Marley circled the same questions around his mind: why did he not have his white father, but did have his white features?

"Sometimes he'd come across the resistance of being half-caste," his wife Rita later said. "There was a problem with his counterparts. Having come through this white father caused such difficulties that he'd want to kill himself and thinking, 'Why am I this person? Why is my father white and not black like everybody else? What did I do wrong?'

"He was lost in that: not being able to have anyone to say it's not your fault, or that there's nothing wrong in being like you are. But that was the atmosphere he came up in, that Trench Town environment where everybody is rough. He had to show them that although he didn't know his father, at least he knew there was a God and he knew what he was feeling.

"Bob had to put up with a lot of resistance. If he wasn't that strong in himself he wouldn't be what he became today. He would be the downtrodden and seen as another half-caste who would never make it."

In the 1950s, Marley watched Jamaica grow independent from his father's homeland, England. Rulers such as Alexander Bustamante claimed a black identity, but only after reaping the harvest of their ability to pass for white.

Marley infused himself with history, listening intently as his teachers told him Christopher Columbus discovered Jamaica when he laid anchor in Discovery Bay in Marley's St. Ann's. England and Spain fought for the lucrative sugar and tobacco island, and the Taina were killed one by one until they ceased to exist.

Marley fell in love with the Maroons and their multi-generational fight against the English, with sons and daughters picking up the resistance as their mothers and fathers died. Nesta read about the Maroon wars, especially the Second Maroon War in the 1770s that sent the proud, unconquered warriors to Nova Scotia. He learned how the Maroons talked in code through horns, and how they killed anyone who revealed the code's secrets.

Marley saw his Jamaica drawn on the same colour lines: whites at the top, browns in the middle, blacks at the bottom. Some of the white elite set black and brown against each other to avoid a united attack. He watched the island seek to build its tourism industry by inviting whites to holiday there. Jamaica's government erected billboards begging the locals to be nice to the visitors.

The Rastas lived on the edge of Marley's mind. They were scary figures, but also enticing. They were proud to be black. They didn't sell themselves out by claiming as much whiteness as possible to get ahead in a corrupt system. They blasted the "sufferation" of the poor and sneered at Babylon's police.

They did it all to a soundtrack inspired by the echoes of Arawak rhythms, the West African talking drums, and European dance music.

Marley dropped out of school at fourteen and tried to become a welder. But he took a metal sliver in the eye and quit, vowing to focus entirely on music.

Curiously, Nesta started calling himself Bob. His father's family rejected him, and yet he took their white English name. His biographer, Timothy White, says he "preferred to be called by his more adult name." But we don't really know why he did it.

Bob Marley began making music with his childhood friends Bunny Livingston and Peter Tosh. Their songs grew in popularity, and they began making money off them.

The boys got to know some Rastas, who suffered vicious violence from political leaders as the police clashed with poor people in places like Trench Town. Many Rastas fought back at the barricades – that's what they called music – by creating songs that shared their world view with people.

They sang about celebrating tolerance, familial relationships with all people, and fighting oppression.

★ ★ ★

In Trench Town, Marley found a creative, critical environment for music making. People played music on the street and strangers would stop, listen, and suggest improvements. "So is always like that with the people: the people in it," he said of his music.

He found a mentor in Joe Higgs, a reggae musician who was about the same age as Marley, but who achieved success earlier. Higgs also mentored Jimmy Cliff, the musical legend who would win global fame with songs like "Many Rivers to Cross," "Hakuna Matata," and "The Harder They Come."

Marley learned to turn ideas into songs that were reborn as ideas in listeners' minds. Higgs spoke for Rastas, against police violence, and for morals. He taught the mechanics of breathing songs to life. "After a while I smoke some ganja, some herb, and get to understand it. Me try to get into de mood whar de moon is blue and see de feelin' expressed," Marley said.

By 1961, Marley, Tosh, and Livingston were calling themselves the Teenagers. They soon changed the name to the Wailing Rudeboys, then the Wailing Wailers, then the Wailers. Tosh explained the progression.

"The word 'wail' means to cry or to moan," he said. "We were living in this so-called ghetto. No one to help the people. We felt we were the only ones who could express their feelings through music, and because of that the people loved it. So did we."

★ ★ ★

The Wailers recorded their first two songs on Marcus Garvey Drive in Trench Town in 1962. One was called "Judge Not," the other "Do You Still Love

Me." Both are upbeat, innocent pop love songs with a light voice zipping along. You would guess 504 other singers before suggesting it was Bob Marley. He left the recording studios with two vinyl records of his newly birthed music, but no access to a record player.

Also in 1962, Jamaica lowered the British flag and raised its own as an independent nation. The new country sought heroes, and so in 1964 Jamaica brought Marcus Garvey home.

Nearly twenty-five years after his lonely London death, Garvey's body was raised out of the crypt and returned to Jamaica. The government declared him a secular saint and interred him with great ceremony in National Heroes Park. His burial vault, made from terrazzo inset with marble, sits in the centre of a black star as tribute to his Black Star Line Shipping Company. A bronze bust captures him in a noble moment.

A year after Garvey was repatriated, Martin Luther King Jr. came to Jamaica with his wife Coretta on a pilgrimage to the shrine. King laid a wreath and spoke of the impact Garvey had on his own life.

"[Garvey] was the first man of colour to lead and develop a mass movement. He was the first man on a mass scale and level to give millions of Negroes a sense of dignity and destiny. And make the Negro feel he was somebody," King said.

* * *

Rebel music sang in Marley's abandoned heart. It started to seep into his pop music. 1964's "Simmer Down" calls for calm among the rude boys. The song was a local hit, selling thousands of copies. It stood out on the charts as a precursor to hip hop's role as the CNN of the ghetto – this was boys from the shantytown singing songs about the shantytown. It was called sufferah, and suddenly it caught airplay. "Simmer Down" went on to sell 70,000 copies in 1964.

Google the cover. It shows three men in tuxedos and shiny shoes. Their short hair is slicked down to the skull. They stand in front of a happy yellow backdrop with a white circle. Two of the men hold hands, making a bridge for Bob, who dives forward happily, smiling under his bright eyes and short hair. It takes a careful staring to recognize the iconic Marley in the youthful celebration. Same for the voice surfing on the ska beat (a precursor to reggae music) suggesting you simmer down and control your temper.

Marley flirted with the idea of claiming his white identity. It certainly offered a better chance of success.

"I'm Still Waiting" sounds like the opposite of Bob Marley, but it was an early hit – a silky, groovy little love song. It was another local hit. In an alternative universe, Bob Marley is today remembered vaguely as an old-time crooner you hear once in a while on the nostalgic radio stations.

The Wailers recorded "It Hurts To Be Alone," a big-heart ballad sung by a man called Junior Braithwaite. The Wailers got spiffy gold jackets and garish shirts. Even in this pre-reggae stage, the Wailers' producer noticed a strange thing. Bob Marley did not work the crowd on stage, like most lead singers. Instead, he went deep inside himself and the people followed him into his vast interior. But despite his strange stage presence, the music still sounded like Jamaica's answer to the "Love Me Do" Beatles.

★ ★ ★

In 1966, at twenty-one, he wed Rita Anderson. Born in Cuba, she grew up in Kingston, Jamaica. Anderson met Marley when she auditioned to join the Soulettes trio singing with the Wailers. The women were later called the I-Threes. In their wedding photo, he smiles in a dark suit and sweater. His hair is still very short. He still struggles with his mixed-race identity.

"Who is me? A fockin' blood-clat'at whit man pickney?" he asked Rita.

"God is your father," she replied. "The father is just sent physically to bring you, but your real father is watching over you and will never disown you."

The day after their wedding, Marley left Rita to see his newly married mother in Wilmington, Delaware. He worked as a waiter, drove a forklift truck, and took a spot on a Chrysler assembly line. He experienced American anti-black racism. He concluded that black people mustn't bow to white people, but must be superior. He asked: If you are superior, how can you be prejudiced?

While he stayed in the U.S., Marley deputized Rita to see Haile Selassie when he landed in Jamaica. Neither Bob nor Rita were Rastas, but both were interested in learning more about it. Rita got dressed up and watched Selassie leave the plane. She converted on the spot, leaving Christianity for Rastafarianism. At the time, it was a black religion centred on a black king seen as the black embodiment of God.

Marley changed, too, growing a small Afro, losing the gold suit, and becoming vegetarian. He decided to move back to Jamaica. With Rita, he studied the Rasta way of life with its focus on serving the poor and outcast.

"Him learn so much from the experience of people who suffer. Bob was taught in a Rasta university. And him understood well. Him a bright student," said one teacher, Mortimo Planno.

★ ★ ★

Marley and his wife briefly moved to Delaware and he worked again at the car factory, but then got served notice to register for the draft. That could mean fighting in Vietnam. He left America in 1968.

When he got home, he rolled a joint and got high enough to gain a perspective on his fledgling career. When he came down, he fully embraced Rastafarianism and his black identity. Marley's white half was entirely subjugated. He started to read Garvey, to learn about his Back to Africa vision, his confidence in his race. No matter how you thrive in chains, freedom is better. And freedom meant Africa. Rastas debated whether it was physical Africa or spiritual Africa.

He listened to other bands. Young musicians slowed the ska beat down, halved the rhythm, and stepped up the bass and drum. Duke Reid's "Rock Steady" shows the new sound. The political mood got serious, too. The country had changed, and Bob Marley changed. Listen to "Bend Down Low," and now you hear the Marley millions would love: a slow, hypnotic furrow planting seeds that would grow into higher things. "It's Alright" followed the idea deeper. Bob Marley had found his voice.

He found his hair, too, sprouting springy dreadlocks. Rastas taught that "no razor shall come upon his head until the days be fulfilled, in which he separateth himself unto the Lord, he shall be holy, and shall let the locks of the hair of his head grow," as the Book of Numbers explained it.

* * *

In 1967, the Wailers released "Hypocrites," "Nice Time," and "Pyaka." Rita preached Rasta to him, telling and retelling how she saw Haile Selassie when he visited in 1966. All around him, ghetto boys grew out their hair in spiky locks.

Marley spent time with the Rasta leader Mortimo Planno, the man who had greeted Selassie in Jamaica. He sat with Rastas over nights, listening to their music, smoking their marijuana, hearing their reasoning. Marley talked about his driving need to write songs – but not pop songs to sell vinyl. He wanted to create trench-deep songs to redeem black souls.

Planno enticed him into a Rasta world view, talking of Egypt's great black kings, and the sacred herb they smoked for enlightenment. The reasoning session went deep into the nights, and back into the days.

Listen to the new sound, with the old lyrics, in "Milkshake and Potato Chips," a reggae song about a woman who eats too many snacks.

* * *

Marley poured music and religion into the father-shaped hole inside. His father haunted him in dreams, one time appearing in a military uniform and old fedora. The supernatural captain gave dreaming Marley a gold ring set with a small diamond in onyx. "This is all I have to give you," father told son. Ciddy later found the ring – Norval had given it to her – and she gave it to Marley.

"I felt Bob wasn't secure in himself at this time," said Benjamin Foot, who would become his tour manager in England. "I think he was perturbed that one of his parents was white, and he wanted to prove himself very much as being a black Rasta."

The youthful rebellion against the sting of rejection set him on a deep journey into the human experience.

★ ★ ★

Bob Marley began to convert from Christianity to Rastafarianism by the mid-1960s, and by the late '60s let its world view take over his mind. Perhaps his first Rasta-infused song was "One Love" in 1965, centring on the call to unity and echoing Garvey's unity cry from a generation before.

He followed Garvey's physical and intellectual trail to London. Marley befriended members of the Ethiopian Royal family living there. Crown Prince Afsa Wossen, son of Haile Selassie, gave him a ring. It featured a gold Lion of Judah set in onyx, and Marley never let that ring off his hand. The gesture showed a profound internal shift: Marley rejected his absent white father for a mystical black father. Author Gregory Stephens called Selassie Marley's "perfect African father."

"Marley was in some sense the fulfillment of Malcolm X's late advice that the 'back to Africa' movement, which Garvey and others had advocated, should be read and enacted as a cultural turn, rather than a physical return," writes Stephens.

Songs like "Exodus" and "Survival" urge a return to our father's land. Marley talked about leaving Babylon (code for the West) and returning to Zion or the Promised Land (both code for Africa). "The dream of Africa as homeland that he portrayed as Zion was the resolution of or redemption from its opposite: Babylon," Stephens explains.

Babylon also refers to a state of mind: self-obsessed, idol-worshiping, idle people sitting on a mountain of poverty and eating grapes. We humans need to leave Babylon (by bus or other means) and travel to Zion. In an article called "The Influence of Bob Marley's Absent White Father," Scott Gurtman argues that Marley described a physical Zion because the absence of his father drove him to see Selassie as a real substitute as father, hence the need to focus on a real, physical place – Ethiopia. The exodus to Africa represents the journey to spiritual and psychological peace.

* * *

As his music career took off, Marley read voraciously: the Bible, music magazines, and Marcus Garvey. During the 1978 *Kaya* tour, he turned to Malcolm X and Angela Davis to deepen his black identity.

Scott Gurtman asks a simple question: Why did Marley portray himself (and see himself) as a black man, rather than as a man half black, and half white? You could ask further why most of us see him the same way. For that matter, look at the famous photo of U.S. President Barack Obama sitting on a bench with his white grandparents.

Gurtman concludes that Marley was by the late

1970s comfortable with himself, and his identity, and sought to deepen his legacy as a freedom fighter. But also, Gurtman thinks, it was Marley's final dismissal of Norval Marley, returning his father's rejection.

And while he became a powerful figure for black people, he found his biggest audience among white people. Asked about this, Marley said there should be no more war between black and white. But until white people listen to black people with open ears, there must be suspicion.

Another time, he said, "Is God who make everybody, and him make a way for the black man that the white man have to follow, because out of the black man came the white man, all me.

"Me only have one ambition, you know. I only have one thing I really like to see happen. I like to see mankind live together – black, white, Chinese, everyone – that's all."

To understand what Marley's saying, we must first understand what the Rastas were telling him.

Song 18:
"The man of sorrows ain't nothing else but a coloured man."

In November 1930, the serene face of Haile Selassie dominated the cover of *Time* magazine. "With the cross of Jesus on his breast, Tafari Makonnen, already King of Kings, Conquering Lion of Judah and the Elect of God, proceeded last week to his Second Coronation, this time as Power of Trinity the First, Emperor of Ethiopia," *Time*'s reporter wrote.

Actually, he missed one title: His Imperial Majesty. After comparing his physical appearance to a "Spanish Jew," the article said that "throughout the world last week Negro news organs hailed him as their own."

National Geographic made him the cover story, pouring praise on the African ruler in a way that shocked its readers. England's Prince Henry, Duke of Gloucester and son of King George V, attended his coronation. Italy sent the Prince of Uldine. France sent Marshal Louis Franchet d'Esperey, hero of the Great War.

Here was Ethiopia reaching out her hands to the world. For Garveyites, it made flesh the theory that black is beautiful. It proved God is black.

That's the central belief of Rastafarianism. Generations of Christians heard that God created humans in his image, and all the images on the church walls were white men and women. Jesus was a white man. Mary was a white woman. All the saints were white. All the ministers were white. Therefore, God was white.

Prester John, the black Christian king of the east, vanished. Saint Maurice turned white.

The Rastas turned God black.

The beginning of understanding Rastafarianism lies in the name. As we saw earlier, Ras Tafari comes from two words: *ras* means head or prince, and *tafari* means he who inspires awe. Ras Tafari is a title meaning the prince who inspires awe.

Haile Selassie became Ethiopia's Earthly ruler after the death of the Empress Zewditu in 1930, and soon took on a global role comparable to a combination of Nelson Mandela and the Dalai Lama. He traced his roots to Menelik I, child of King Solomon and Queen Sheba.

The handsome, regal ruler's home country, Ethiopia, then stood for black power – the lone African country well regarded by Europe, famous around the globe, and coming from a venerable history. It's one of the brutal ironies of life that today "Ethiopia" for Westerners means famine and hunger, and rock singers holding fundraisers to feed the world. For Marcus

Garvey, for Bob Marley, and for Rastafarians, Ethiopia meant feasts, wealth, dignity, and African power.

Starting in Jamaica in the 1930s, Rastas saw more: they saw a messianic figure, a prophet, and finally the biblical God incarnate. Jah – God's proper name from the Hebrew letters YHWH (this also gives us Yahweh).

Before he left Jamaica in 1916, Marcus Garvey issued his prophecy: "Look to Africa for the crowning of a black king. He shall be the redeemer." The highly publicized coronation of Selassie convinced Rastas that he was Jesus come again, and Garvey had been his John the Baptist.

Before taking the crown, Selassie travelled through the Middle East, Europe, and Africa. "We need European progress only because we are surrounded by it. That is at once a benefit and a misfortune," he said. He travelled with a pride of lions and astonished Europe, just as the legend of Prester John had in the Middle Ages. In Jerusalem, he adopted forty Armenian orphans who had lost their parents to Ottoman massacres. He had them taught music and they eventually formed his imperial brass band.

Selassie ruled as Emperor of Ethiopia and when Italian fascists attacked in 1936, he fought back hard. The world – especially the black diaspora – watched in awe as this African emperor went toe to toe with a great European power. Rome versus Addis Ababa.

Ethiopia had won the first Italo-Abyssinian War in 1896. Anyone who did not fight in the second war would "be rebuked for it by your Creator and will be cursed by your offspring," Selassie said. Italy launched chemical attacks and bombed Red Cross hospitals. The modern European army invaded, but ran into stiff opposition. Italy advanced over fields of dead Ethiopians. Selassie fled and took his case to the League of Nations. He asked for help standing up to the fascists.

"It is collective security: it is the very existence of the League of Nations. It is the confidence that each State is to place in international treaties," he told the League leaders. "In a word, it is international morality that is at stake. Have the signatures appended to a treaty value only in so far as the signatory powers have a personal, direct and immediate interest involved?"

He became a global icon in the worldwide fight against fascism and against European colonial rule.

On Christmas 1937, two months after Garvey's historic Sydney address, Selassie took to the radio to address the American people. "With the birth of the Son of God, an unprecedented, an unrepeatable, and a long-anticipated phenomenon occurred. He was born in a stable instead of a palace, in a manger instead of a crib. The hearts of the Wise Men were struck by fear and wonder due to His Majestic Humbleness. The kings prostrated themselves before Him and worshipped Him. 'Peace be to those who have good will.' This became the first message," Selassie told them.

"Although the toils of wise people may earn them respect, it is a fact of life that the spirit of the wicked continues to cast its shadow on this world. The arrogant are seen visibly leading their people into crime and destruction. The laws of the League of Nations are constantly violated and wars and acts of aggression repeatedly take place … So that the spirit of the cursed will not gain predominance over the human race whom Christ redeemed with his blood, all peace-loving people should cooperate to stand firm in order to preserve and promote lawfulness and peace."

Rastas took it as code for his revelation that he was indeed the second coming of Christ.

In 1941, with British backing he re-entered Ethiopia and raised the Lion of Judah flag. On May 5, 1941, he triumphed into Addis Ababa and retook his throne. "Take care not to spoil the good name of Ethiopia by acts which are worthy of the enemy. We shall see that our enemies are disarmed and sent out the same way they came," he said.

In 1942, he abolished slavery from Ethiopia. In 1947, he sent aid to Britain after a bad flood. In 1963, he mourned at President John Kennedy's funeral.

★ ★ ★

Many Jamaican Rastas who watched film of the splendid coronation, and subsequent footage of the global hero, understood Selassie was the predicted African messiah sent to redeem slavery's diaspora.

In 1963, he solidified his standing with his War Speech to the UN. He returned to Ethiopia and gave the same message. "Throughout history, it has been the inaction of those who could have acted; the indifference of those who should have known better; the silence of the voice of justice when it mattered most; that has made it possible for evil to triumph," he said.

He visited Jamaica in 1966 – that's when Rita Marley saw him disembark the airplane and converted. Some 100,000 Rastafaris gathered to see him. He entered the island through a haze of ganja smoke. He told them to liberate Jamaica before thinking of a return to Africa. "Liberation before repatriation," he said.

He seemed to accept his role as the returned Jesus Christ. He met with Rasta elders and gave them gold medallions. A CBC reporter asked him if he was God.

"I have heard of that idea. I also met certain Rastafarians. I told them clearly that I am a man, that I am mortal, and that I will be replaced by the oncoming generation, and that they should never make a mistake in assuming or pretending that a human being is emanated from a deity."

But Jesus said similar things, so Selassie's denial didn't deter the faithful.

His visit marked a turning point. Rastas focused on life at home, rather than in the ancestral home.

Rasta practitioners developed a theology for the poor, illiterate people packed into cheap housing. It developed Dread Talk as a way to speak against police violence, political oppression, and corrupt judiciary. Dread Talk used code names. Babylon stood for oppression and Zion for redemption.

They used speech-acts to bring the plight of the poor to ordinary Jamaicans. They built pride and taught people to rely on themselves, to grow food for themselves, to seek their own emancipation.

"They contend that the poor must liberate themselves. They must create their own history," Noel Leo Erskine writes in *From Garvey to Marley: Rastafari Theology*.

Rastas urged the oppressed to untrust the oppressor class to improve their lives. Those who benefit from the Babylon system do not truly want to change it, the Rasta man said. Middle- and upper-class Jamaicans largely turned their backs on the movement.

★ ★ ★

At the start, Rastas subscribed to the ideology of racism – that humans exist in distinct races, which are hereditary and inflexible. Like Garvey, the black Rastas believed it was time for the black race to chuck off the white race's oppression and build a rival, free, black country. Every race must find a home: Ireland for the Irish, Africa for the Africans.

Both Garvey and Selassie were Christians, so Rastas followed the Bible and built a new religion out of it, much like early Christians and Muslims founded new faiths out of Judaism.

Rastas knew most people saw God as white. To see yourself in the face of God, God has to look like you. So they used Garvey to go beyond Garvey and see Haile Selassie as a black God.

Garvey spoke about the colour of God at a 1924 UNIA convention. Garvey didn't say God was black, but he did say that humans see God through human eyes, and black people saw God through black eyes. "We Negroes believe in the God of Ethiopia. We shall worship him through the spectacles of Ethiopia," he said.

"The man of sorrows ain't nothing else but a coloured man," replied a man from Mississippi.

Most Rastas came to agree with the Mississippian. As Garvey turned to middle-class America and Jamaica to fund his Black Star Line, Rastas stayed with the poor. Garvey and his Garveyites went a different way, but Rastas continued to turn to 1920s Garvey as a prophet. Garvey certainly never saw Selassie as a god or as God. But Rastas saw him as a prophet, and prophets can make mistakes. By paving the way for Selassie, he had completed his mission. Rastas turned from Garvey to Selassie.

The seed of Garveyism bloomed independently into Rastafari.

* * *

Ethiopia remained the Promised Land. Garvey himself called it the Land of our Fathers. Rastas see it as the Zion spoken of in the Bible. The Exodus of Africans would return to that Zion.

Rastas turned away from the Babylon system, that vampire sucking the blood of the sufferers. Black businesses, white businesses, it was all the same Babylon system. The rebel Rastas sought a new way of life entirely.

Leonard Percival Howell, a former Garveyite, became the main founder of Rastafarianism after the coronation of Selassie. Howell and his Rastas withdrew from Babylon into the high place of Pinnacle, the first Rasta community.

Like mystics and monks of old, they changed their appearance to signal their withdrawal from worldly concerns. They wore dreads, smoked herb, and moved to an internal Zion. Here, the Seven Principles of Rastafari were laid down. They believed that:

> Haile Selassie is the returning God spoken of in Revelations.
>
> Marcus Garvey showed the way out of bondage.
>
> Rastas must fight oppression.

Ethiopia is the Holy Land.

Rastas must seek repatriation to Africa. (Rastas soon modified this to making pilgrimage to Africa, not necessarily moving there. When Selassie "disappeared" in the 1970s, Rastas evolved this belief further so that you could be Rasta, and African, in Jamaica, or wherever you happened to be born.)

Live naturally. Rastas became vegetarians and sought simple, monkish lives.

Reason with other people. Rastas carry a Bible in one hand and a newspaper in the other. Elders may offer sermons on the faith, but then everybody gathers for a reasoning session to share their own thoughts and collectively approach the mysteries. Reason shaped by revelation becomes wisdom.

Pinnacle became like the River Jordan, the place you went for baptismal transformation. Some five hundred Rastas lived amid the fields of marijuana. Police raided Pinnacle in 1954, destroyed the community, and had Howell committed to an asylum.

★★★

With its deep focus on African pride, there are few non-black Rastas and much debate if a white Rasta could exist.

Many Rastas looked away when Selassie emerged as a tyrant, crushing political opposition and triggering famines. Problems were apparent before he took the throne, and continued after he was reinstalled.

Human Rights Watch records that in 1968, Selassie sent his air force to bomb villages and burn houses to intimidate the resistance.

Selassie tried to hide famines in 1958, 1966, and 1972. Human Rights Watch says the locals "were treated with official indifference, bordering on hostility towards the peasants who were considered sufficiently ungrateful for the divinely sanctioned rule of Haile Selassie as to allow themselves to defame his reputation by dying of famine."

But Bob Marley still put large portraits of Selassie – and Garvey – on the back of his stages as he toured the world, still praised the man Rastas knew to be God.

To Rastas, the Bible was written by black people for black people. It's not an authority, though, but a starting point for the reasoning that leads to wisdom. Rastas saw themselves as Israelites, and the themes of being sold into slavery and seeking an exodus resonated. These beliefs deeply influenced Marley's music and would soon lead him to write "Redemption Song."

Song 19:
"We call ourselves the Wailers because we started out crying."

As 1969 turned into 1970, Marley went into Scratch Perry's open-door studio. Musicians strolled in and out of the Wailers' sessions. Street people brought street tales like the crazed story of a crow named Mr Brown riding coffins through town, riding his way right into the Wailers' song "Mr. Brown."

Like Garvey, Marley stuck himself to the streets, and the streets heard itself in his voice. *Soul Rebels* came in 1970. *Soul Revolution* followed.

Marley wound up in Stockholm, Sweden, recording music for a movie that died a short death, and redoing an old song called "Stir It Up." He wrote the song for Rita, whose father lived in Stockholm. Leroy Anderson left Jamaica to marry a Finn, have two kids, and drive a midnight taxi through Stockholm. Two black men in Scandinavia in the 1960s stood out, and they soon met for the first time. Marley lived in a basement, spooked and hallucinating.

A package of weed was mailed to Marley's house, detected by customs, and nearly wrecked his life with jail time in Europe. A friend took the blame and Marley flew home, and flew to Chris Blackwell, the white man who ran Island Records. Blackwell was already seeking a rock-reggae rebel to carry the torch for the music.

As a boy, Blackwell tipped out of a boat and nearly drowned. He made it to shore, where Rastas rescued him, tended his wounds, and taught him about love. So when dread-full Marley came to his door, he knew what he was about. The band signed with Blackwell's Island Records and released *Catch a Fire*, whose single "Concrete Jungle" brought Marley to an international audience.

A strange Englishman dressed as a king introduced them on the British TV staple, *The Old Grey Whistle Test*. Marley closed his eyes, opened his mind, and brought millions of strangers to his tough Jamaican streets with "Concrete Jungle," then lightened into "Stir It Up."

As Timothy White notes in his book *Catch a Fire*, in 1973 the "white, middle-class American rock journal *Rolling Stone* handed down its verdict on *Catch a Fire*," calling it a "mature, fully realized sound with a beautiful lyric sensibility."

Marley started to reach a huge new audience. He knew his music wasn't novelty "world" music from the slums of a third-world island, but a deep, spinal sound resonating in the ears of sufferers around the planet. "We begin like them people in the Bible, who go on Exodus. We call ourselves the Wailers because we started out crying," he explained.

The Wailers played London. The show drew Bianca Jagger, Bryan Ferry, and Brian Eno to the packed Speakeasy. The musicians instantly saw the Wailers were special. No rock star crotch grabs, no working the audience – just three men playing deep inside their souls.

"I don't come to bow. I come to conquer," was how Marley put it.

The Wailers played in Blackpool, a working-class northern English town, and yet somehow connected to the crowd. Marley may have rejected his English father, but England embraced her prodigal son.

"It was the white audience in Britain who took Bob up first, really. The Rastas got into him later," said Dennis Morris, a Jamaican-born English kid who voluntarily travelled with the Wailers on that tour.

"Chris Blackwell had put him into that cross-over market, and white people were the first to pick up on it. Later, of course, Bob had a huge black audience, but they seemed to misinterpret what Bob was personally saying about Rasta, and read it as just being a black thing, a black power thing almost. But to me Bob always insisted, 'It's the system we're against – it's not a black and white thing.'"

Meanwhile, Jamaican radio stations worked back-door deals with record companies and played their hits, but ignored the Wailers.

Then it snowed in Europe and the frozen Wailers left, vowing never to play a winter tour again in Babylon.

★ ★ ★

Natty Dread came out in 1974 and the Wailers re-formed around the I-Threes, the singing trio of Rita Marley, Judy Mowatt, and Marcia Griffiths. Griffiths was already a music star, well-known for her duet with Bob Andy called "Young, Gifted and Black." Mowatt had enjoyed success with the Gaylettes before joining the I-Threes.

The group's live shows were turning the music into a movement. "Bob held the audience as though they were part of his collective soul," Adrian Boot and Chris Salewicz write in *Bob Marley: Songs of Freedom*. "He could have told them to go out into the street and to burn and loot and they would have obeyed him."

But that's not what he wanted them to do. The celebrated London show in the Lyceum Ballroom on July 18, 1975, broke the band wide open. Starting with a menacing version of "Burnin' and Lootin'," the show brought the English audience singalong versions of "No Woman No Cry" and "I Shot the Sheriff." That last one had recently been covered by Eric Clapton.

"From that gig, every person who was there decided they were a Rasta, and it snowballed. The whole movement just spread," said Dennis Morris. The first tour brought 1,500 people, the next 5,000, then 10,000. Sweden and England were the two biggest early backers.

"I live a long time before me see any money, but my work here is not to become a 'star' or anything like that, and my life no go toward material vanity. I find myself doing this music t'ing and me have to do it. Really, I am just a man of the heart," Marley told an interviewer as the band's fame grew.

"The first thing you must know about me is that I always stand what I stand for. Good? The second thing you must know about yourself listening to me is that words are tricky. So when you know what me a stand for, when me explain a thing to you, you must never try to look 'pon it in a different way from what me a stand for."

By the time *Natty Dread* dropped, Chris Blackwell had spent more than $500,000 on Bob Marley. He remained confident of a breakthrough that would regain him that money. Marley clashed with his old friend Pete Tosh. Tosh said Marley had succeeded mainly because he was half white.

★ ★ ★

Marley spent more time playing England. His father, grandfather, and great-grandfather all came from England. The Wailers toured the U.S., bouncing over gentle groves, telling the white audiences that the tables were turned on the slave-driver, who was bound to burn in hell.

Among the wild culture of the 1970s, these biblical prophets stuck as something else. Sly and the Family Stone hired the Wailers to open for them, but then fired them because it felt like Sly was closing for Marley. Even the other Wailers found themselves sliding backwards as the band was renamed Bob Marley and the Wailers.

The *Burnin'* album took Marley deeper into songs that sounded like old Negro spirituals recently uncovered: "Get Up, Stand Up," "Duppy Conqueror," and "Rastaman Chant." The record's front featured stencils of the Wailers burning through wood planks; the reverse showed a silhouette of Marley launching a joint the size of a cigar. The inside displays photos of Trench Town, showing the music of the ghetto, the landscape where echoed the weeping and wailing that accompanied the burning and looting.

"A lot of people believed that a Mau Mau-inspired cult of demonic anti-white murderers had been uncovered in the Caribbean. The music conjured up images of white tourists being hacked to death on the fringes of tropical golf courses," White writes.

And yet white people were still drawn to this Black Power champion. What did Marley think as he sang about black is beautiful, about Africa, and when he flickered his eyes open and peered between his growing dreadlocks, he saw a sea of white faces singing it back to him?

Paul McCartney became a fan. So did Mick Jagger. So did Paul Simon. *Natty Dread* rolled onward in 1974, blazing out legends such as "Lively Up Yourself," "Them Belly Full (But We Hungry)," "Rebel Music," and the gigantic "No Woman No Cry."

Haile Selassie, Marley's adopted black father, died in 1975. Many wondered what it meant for the future of Rastafarianism, now that Jah was dead. Marley went to the studio to write and release his answer: "Jah Live!"

What he heard in his mind, and shared from his mouth, was the secret vibration of many hearts. Those hearts drove their feet to the record store and bought the single, making the Wailers international stars.

* * *

Rastaman Vibration was released in 1976 putting Marley's beliefs at the centre of his music. Island Records brought the press to Marley, creating a pilgrimage route for European and North American journalists to study his mystic persona. White describes how the poverty and roughness of Kingston "turned their pale faces alabaster."

Marley, meanwhile, joined a Rasta group called the Twelve Tribes of Israel, an otherworldly outfit gathered around a Trench Town man called Vernon Carrington and preparing for serene repatriation to Ethiopia's Goba Valley. Kingston police expressed their opinions by forcibly cutting the dreads off eighty Rastas. The back of the *Rastaman Vibration* album showed the Blessing of Joseph, a covert reference to Marley's new Rasta identity. Each "tribe" had its colour, and interestingly Marley's colour was white.

He wrote Rasta prophets directly into songs, for example setting a celebrated Selassie speech to music in "War." Selassie, also known as Emperor Menelik II, stood before the United Nations in 1963 and laid out his case as he explained his former fight with the fascists of Italy, and his way forward for peace. It's a long speech, but worth quoting this excerpt as it will be familiar to Marley fans.

"Until the philosophy which holds one race superior and another inferior is finally and permanently discredited and abandoned; that until there are no longer first-class and second-class citizens of any nation; that until the colour of a man's skin is of no more significance than the colour of his eyes; that until the basic human rights are equally guaranteed to all without regard to race; that until that day, the dream of lasting peace and world citizenship and the rule of international morality will remain but a fleeting illusion, to be pursued but never attained;

"And until the ignoble and unhappy regimes that hold our brothers in Angola, in Mozambique and in South Africa in subhuman bondage have been toppled and destroyed; until bigotry and prejudice and malicious and inhuman self-interest have been replaced by understanding and tolerance and good-will; until all Africans stand and speak as free beings, equal in the eyes of all men, as they are in the eyes of Heaven; until that day, the African continent will not know peace. We Africans will fight, if necessary, and we know that we shall win, as we are confident in the victory of good over evil."

Like all Rastas, Marley kept a newspaper in one hand and holy scriptures in the other. He used his music to fuse the two worlds.

★ ★ ★

Marley lived in a big house on Hope Road about an hour's walk from Trench Town. Jamaica's political factions clashed in the streets ahead of a national election in 1976 and Marley intended to play at the Smile Jamaica peace concert. Getting involved in politics, even in a non-partisan way, brought the violence to his home.

"People see him as a big man now, gone international," his friend Mikey Smith told journalist Vivien Goldman. "Everyone want Bob Marley deh 'pon their team."

Goldman spoke to Marley just before his home was attacked and recounts their conversation in her

1981 book *Bob Marley, Soul Rebel – Natural Mystic*.

"People work for money, den dem don't want to split it. It's that kind of attitude. So much guys have so much – too much – while so many have nothing at all. We don't feel that is right, because it don't take a guy a hundred million dollars to keep him satisfied," he told her in late 1976.

"We need a change from what it was. It couldn't get worse than that. You have to share. I don't care if it sounds political or whatever it is, but people have to share."

That "socialist" perspective led some to conclude he supported Michael Manley's People's National Party, linked to Cuba and the Soviet Union, and rejected Edward Seaga's Jamaican Labour Party.

Marley invited people to his house and often shared food, money, and marijuana. On the night of December 3, 1976, Rita Marley drove through the house's main gates and let another car in. A passenger in that car shot her in the head. Three gunmen ran into the kitchen and opened fire.

Marley watched a bullet rip over his heart and strike his arm. "Indeed, even though this was the moment Bob had been dreading, when the shock came, he froze. Everything went into slow motion," Goldman writes. Marley's entourage chased the gunmen out and soon the police arrived. Rita Marley was treated for superficial wounds, but was traumatized by the attack.

Uncowed, Marley played the Smile Jamaica concert. Despite the grim mood and threat of assassins Marley took the stage in front of a pulsating crowd of 80,000 people, throwing his dreads in undreading triumph. He hit the crowd with "War/No More Trouble." Rita stood on stage with him.

YouTube videos of the concert show him burning deeply inward, singing like it's coming straight from Jah – which it was. It was the War Speech Selassie gave to the UN, set to reggae, turned into poetry.

"Until that day, the African continent shall have no peace. We Africans will fight if necessary. We know we shall win," he told the thousands.

Marley ended the song with a hunting dance from Ethiopia. Traditionally, warriors danced it before the emperor to show how they had stepped toward death and seized victory. Marley bared his chest and arm to show the bullet wounds, showing how he defeated death for another day. He left the stage laughing with the gods.

* * *

Towards the end of his life, he bought Rita a massive house in the toniest region of Kingston. They had wealthy, well-connected, powerful neighbours. One of them was the Marley family, Bob's paternal kin. He never spoke publicly about why he chose that house, or if he ever reconciled with his father's family.

* * *

The Bible says the Jews were enslaved in Egypt in ancient times. Moses led them out to the wilderness, where they wandered for forty years, including up Mount Sinai for the Ten Commandments. He eventually took them to the edge of the Promised Land.

Rastas, reading the Bible in one hand and newspapers in the other, saw the same story playing out for Africans. They too had been enslaved, taken from the homeland, and trapped. They too needed an exodus to get home after four hundred years in the wilderness.

Marley explored that theme in 1977 with *Exodus: Movement of Jah People*. The title track ripped across North America and brought Marley a huge new audience, especially among black North Americans. Marley told the world he was leaving Babylon and going to his father's land.

As this wave of international success broke under his feet, he hurt a toe playing soccer. It healed slowly. Doctors discovered he had skin cancer and it was spreading from his foot. They advised him to amputate the toe, but Rastas didn't approve of mutilation, so Marley declined. He made peace with approaching death and predicted he would die as Jesus did, at age thirty-six.

In 1978, Jamaicans hoping to tamp down political fighting organized the Once Love Peace concert. The Wailers would draw big crowds and the money would go to improving life in the slums of Kingston. Less than a week before the concert, police killed three people protesting against slum conditions.

Marley and the Wailers wrote and launched a new record to go with the show: *Kaya*. But *Kaya* didn't capture the public mood of anger. Instead, it's a tranquil exploration of kaya, or marijuana. The anger of *Exodus* yields to the soothing groove of peace and love with songs including "Satisfy My Soul," "Is This Love," "Time Will Tell," and "Kaya."

Critics said Marley had gone soft and forgotten the concrete jungle.

Marley created a peace at the concert, though, bringing leaders from the rival parties on stage to shake hands. After the show, he thought about fusing the angry energy of *Exodus* with the spiritual peace of *Kaya*. He flipped through the newspapers with one hand and held the Bible in the other. He ignited the holy herb, the wisdom weed, and started to compose "Redemption Song."

Song 20:
Marijuana: The Healing of the Nation

Chinese emperor Shen Neng loved to get high and encouraged his subjects to smoke marijuana for medical use. Back in 2737 B.C., Neng got so high that he imagined he could look through his skin to see inside his stomach. He thought it let him better understand marijuana's beneficial behaviour.

The ancient Chinese used it mainly as a medicine, but soon discovered its trippy effects and lit up recreationally. They may be the first people who got high for pleasure and exploration.

The happy plant was popular in the ancient world: Scythians smoked herb at funerals, while Thracians threw it into a fire, huffed it, and fell asleep.

Around 100 A.D., Chinese Taoists started smoking pot in huge amounts. The monks got so high they saw the path to immortality. "The Taoists must have been quite motivated," Mitch Earleywine notes in *Understanding Marijuana*, as it took them one hundred days of hotboxing to get there.

Hindus knew that the god Shiva brought marijuana down from the Himalayas for the faithful to enjoy. Mothers in ancient Jerusalem used it during childbirth, Indian healers deployed it to fight coughs, asthma, and leprosy, while Cambodian women still use it to reduce post-partum depression. Archeologists dug up seven-hundred-year-old pot pipes on a recent excavation in Ethiopia.

More recent medical research has found it can combat blindness caused by glaucoma, stave off the effects of post-traumatic stress disorder, and ease chronic pain.

So why are there laws against marijuana in every country on earth?

The trouble started in 1090 when Persian missionary Hasan-ibn-Sabah led a band of zealots called the Assassins. According to rumour, the zealots smoked drugs to inspire their atrocities. When explorer Marco Polo brought the tale to Europe in the mid-1200s, he added the imagined fact that the drug in question was marijuana, or hashish. People started to think marijuana induced violent rages. The word "assassins" is a corruption of the word hashish.

The British Indian Hemp Drugs Commission reported in 1894 that "moderate use practically produces no ill effects" and evidence "shows most clearly how little injury society has hitherto sustained from hemp drugs."

In 1908, Canada's Opium Act made opium the first illegal drug in the country. Canada added cocaine in 1911 and, with no parliamentary debate or public conversation, it added marijuana in 1923. It seems

Canada was the very first country to make marijuana illegal.

Nobody knows why. Few people smoked it, or even knew what it was. No scientific research found faults in it. The Canadian prime minister at the time, William Lyon Mackenzie King, regularly attended séances to talk to his dead mother, Leonardo da Vinci, and several of his deceased dogs. But there's no evidence he did so thanks to marijuana.

In 1936, America gave the myth new life in the sensational *Reefer Madness* movie, calling it "the burning weed with its roots in hell" as a cymbal crashes. Allegedly high people start killing loved ones, jumping to their deaths, and going insane in a high-energy rage that is quite funny to watch on YouTube when you're high.

"Although the belief that cannabis causes violence remains, laboratory research reveals that marijuana actually decreases aggression," Earleywine writes.

Some Americans associated the plant with the Mexican immigrants who brought it across the border in the early 1900s. Anti-Mexican racism took the form of anti-marijuana laws. For dramatic effect, officials used the Spanish spelling marihuana. Halifax police still call it "marihuana" in news releases announcing seizures, as if to emphasize the scary foreignness of the plant. So does Health Canada. In 2015, Prime Minister Stephen Harper said the plant was "infinitely worse" than tobacco, but offered no evidence.

A 1998 paper prepared for the Parliament of Canada says despite the stigma, 23 per cent of Canadians have used cannabis. "The most widely used illicit drug is marijuana, which causes relatively few harms for its level of use," wrote the author, Dr. Diane Riley.

Like many mystics of old, Rastas used marijuana as a sacred herb. Marley usually called it "the healing of the nation," and used it for reasoning sessions. Christians turn to wine for sacred ceremonies; Rastas use herb.

"Eat every herb of the land," the Book of Exodus implores, and Rastas obey. It starts with a prayer: "Glory be to the father and to the maker of creation. As it was in the beginning, is now and ever shall be, world without end: Jah Rastafari, Eternal God Selassie I."

Marley said it gave him time to think, a little break from the busy day. He didn't like alcohol, as it "doesn't make you meditate" but drunk. He used marijuana to expand his consciousness, to think through Rasta teachings, and to better understand his role in life. "You can't tell God it's not legal," he once said.

"The more you accept herb, the more you accept Rastafari," Marley said.

People are increasingly accepting marijuana. Returning to the plant's roots, it's legal as medicine across Canada and entirely legal in some U.S. states. Portugal decriminalized all illegal drugs in 2001 and treated usage as a public health issue, not a criminal matter. A 2015 report in the U.K. *Independent* found overdoses from all drugs dropped to three people per million citizens; the European Union average is 17.3.

In 2013, Justin Trudeau admitted he smokes marijuana, inhales it, presumably gets high, and said he's done it as a Member of Parliament. "We had a few good friends over for a dinner party … and one of our friends lit a joint and passed it around. I had a puff," he told reporters.

He also promised to legalize marijuana if he was elected prime minister. Canadians handed him a majority government in the 2015 election. In 2016, he put MP Bill Blair – the former Toronto police chief – in charge of legalizing marijuana in Canada. Blair had spent much of his career buying sacks of marijuana as an undercover cop.

"Simply dealing with marijuana with a criminal sanction and a criminal sanction alone wasn't achieving what we wanted to do," Blair told the *Toronto Star* in a January 8, 2016, article.

"It wasn't keeping it out of the hands of kids; it wasn't preventing organized crime from controlling its distribution and sale in our neighbourhoods; it wasn't reducing the violence and victimization that takes place in poor neighbourhoods; it didn't address the disparity of the impact of that law enforcement that takes place in minority communities much more than in majority communities."

So fittingly, it looks like Canada might now become the first country in the world to legalize the recreational use of marijuana. Fitting for the birthplace of "Redemption Song."

Song 21:
Bob Marley's Nova Scotia Song

After *Exodus*, Marley's musical mood deepened. Judy Mowatt, on stage as one of the I-Threes, described the experience.

"It was like a crusade, a mission. We were like sentinels, like lights. On tour the shows were like church: Bob delivering his sermon. There were mixed emotions in the audience. You could see people literally crying, people in a frenzy, on a spiritual high. I remember one night in Canada a woman gave birth in the audience. These concerts were powerful and highly spiritual.

"There was a power that pulled you there. It was a clean feeling. You leave a concert feeling as though you have learned something, you have gained something. For months, and maybe years, it stays with you."

Marley toiled through the night, listening back to concerts, writing new songs as he travelled. The first time anyone ever heard "No Woman No Cry," for example, was an acoustic version at three a.m. with Marley strumming and singing softly to himself.

His entrancing stage shows were as irresistible as the moon tugging the seas. He rejected those who rejected Africa. "If them look on us as an inferior species, we look on them as nothing."

He began to understand how to fuse anger with peace. "I don't come down on you really with blood and fire, earthquakes and lightning, but you must know that within me, all of that exists too."

The band went "outernational," as the Rastas called it.

A reviewer called the Madison Square Garden concerts "peaceful hysteria." In New Zealand, the mighty Maori pilgrimed across the land to see the Wailers and gave Marley a new name: the Redeemer.

Next he hit Japan, receiving a rapturous reception with massive crowds singing along in English. A little girl bowed to him, but he stopped her. "No, no: that's for the almighty God," he told her. Marley struggled to keep his high perspective in the herbless country. A hook-up finally delivered a stash, which the Wailers wailed through on the first night. When that was gone, they got more from U.S. marines stationed nearby.

Ghandi famously died with just ten possessions. Marley could happily have reduced that to five: his herb, his Bible, his photos of Marcus Garvey and of Haile Selassie, and his guitar.

★ ★ ★

In 1978, Marley left the world tour to visit Ethiopia. Surprisingly little information exists about this trip, but perhaps that's not so surprising. When I started writing this book, I didn't know much about Marcus Garvey and was very familiar with Bob Marley. Now, I feel like I know Garvey intimately, but every time I almost grasp Marley, he dissipates into the smoke. We do know his Ethiopia trip inspired the song "Zimbabwe."

In 1979, he played Harlem's legendary Apollo Theatre, where Garvey had preached a generation before. Late at night, Marley went high and found the soul of a new song he was working on, a new kind of song, one about redemption.

"Yeah, me feel good that plenty people is aware that there is something happening. Man can check it out cos I know Rasta grow. I don't see it deteriorate, I watch them and they grow more and more. It might not be in the headlines every day, but dem grow," he told *NME* magazine around that time.

The reporter asked him if his movement was a "race thing."

"No, it's not really a race thing on that sense because a whole heap of people from all nation, kindred and tongue, follow the Rasta movement. Is dat the Bible seh. But is really a black man organization cos the white man nah know about it in that sense," he explained.

"The black man have the knowledge to hold that thing there while the white man him study, fe mek all things a go to space. But some people a go save still and all these people are one people who believe in something, believe in God, fear of true conscience and the works of Ras Tafari."

★ ★ ★

Kaya drove the Wailers on a massive world tour recorded and released as *Babylon By Bus*. Unresting Marley started the next album, hearing the scythe of death slicing the grass at his feet as he sprinted toward his end. In 1979, he played two new songs at a benefit concert raising money for Rasta children: "Ambush in the Night" and "Zimbabwe."

The African country emancipated itself from colonial rule as Rhodesia. Here Marley spelled together the serene songs of *Kaya* with the religious rage of *Exodus*, creating a powerful political call for revolution, set to music that makes you feel the world is a good place.

The songs marched together on the militant 1979 record *Survival* (originally called *Black Survival*): "Africa Unite," "Babylon System," "Survival." The cover drapes itself in forty-eight African flags.

The global elite offered Marley a seat at the entertainer's table, but he overthrew the table, and threw his lot in with the poor, the rebels, those who dreamed of a more equal world. He mesmerized the world playing "Zimbabwe" live on Independence Day in Zimbabwe in 1980, giving that new nation an unofficial national anthem to solace them in the coming storm of post-independence.

Now his dreads hung halfway down his back, a lion's mane knocking around his transfixing closed eyes and pained mouth. Here comes the African proverb to life: Until the lion has his own storyteller, the hunter will always be the hero. Marley declared himself the Lion of Judah's storyteller.

"Now Bob Marley's got no friends but the sufferers," a Rasta elder said.

A new album raced out of his mind as he created as much music as he could before death pulled him into the grave. As record executives offered him more tours, more money, the world and everything in it, Marley retreated.

As biographer Tim White writes, when one music executive explicitly asked him what he wanted, he wanted only one thing: "photos of Haile Selassie's 1931 visit to America."

Uprising rifled out of his soul. Marley drifted from organized Rastas, following his own deep valley, angering those who wished to tame this lion. He took the Ashanti name Osahene, which means Redeemer in the African tongue of his mother's ancestors.

"He was working with an unassuming will that was lifting him to the peak of his powers," White writes.

At concerts, he often covered his eyes while pulsing his love into the audience, and sang with his eyes screwed shut. He slept three hours a night. "Sleep is an escape for fools," he told a worried friend. "I must be about my father's business."

He knew the cancer in his foot had metastasized to his brain, liver, and lungs, and would soon kill him. Hardly anyone else knew.

★ ★ ★

On the *Survival* tour in 1979, Marley began working on a different type of song. With his Bible in one hand, he put a magazine in the other – *Black Man* magazine. He read about Marcus Garvey's 1937 visit to Nova Scotia and read a transcript of the Sydney speech.

One line resonated deeply: "We are going to emancipate ourselves from mental slavery, because whilst others might free the body, none but ourselves can free the mind." Marley played with the words, smoothed them out, and found a sad but unbeaten melody to put them to.

In the studio he worked his musicians desperately. "Real Situation." "Bad Card." "Zion Train." "Forever Loving Jah." The Wailers finished *Uprising*, an album that would be covered in a giant black man with mountainous dreads rising triumphant with the morning sun, and handed it to Island Records.

But Chris Blackwell, the executive who had long worked with Marley, handed it back. He told Marley it needed more. He felt Marley had a song in him that wasn't on the album. Marley smiled. He came back with a new first song, "Coming In From the Cold," and a new last song for the last album of his life.

"Redemption Song."

* * *

At home on Hope Road, he resumed his old life, running with friends on the coast, chatting with boys, and inviting the "mad people" who would pour stream-of-consciousness thoughts into his reasoning session. On Fridays, the ghetto poor lined up outside his house like they did to senators in ancient Rome, seeking his ear and assistance. *Songs of Freedom* reports Marley handed out $20,000 or $40,000 a day at times.

In 1980, the Wailers toured Africa: Gabon, and

then Rhodesia, on its re-birthday as Zimbabwe. Playing in the ruins of the Great Zimbabwe, Solomon and Sheba's big pyramid. En route, Marley found himself sitting in the same airport as Prince Charles, who sought an audience with Marley in the prince's VIP lounge. Marley sent a friendly counteroffer – how about His Royal Highness come down to the regular waiting area and hang out? The prince declined.

They would run into each other again, as the Wailers' first show was set to be in front of the invited dignitaries, which included Charles. The British flag came down, the new Zimbabwe flag went up, and the Wailers were called out to play before the VIP audience.

The ordinary people outside fought to get inside, and the new president Robert Mugabe's security force bombed them with tear gas, which drifted into the stadium. The gas drove the band off stage, leaving entranced Marley dancing alone and singing "I Shot the Sheriff," until he noticed the silence, opened his eyes, then left the stage. He brought the band back out and they ended the concert with "Zimbabwe."

The next day, the Wailers put on a free show for 100,000 ordinary Zimbabweans.

"Me see myself as a revolutionary who don't have no help and take no bribe from no one and fight it single-handed – with music," Marley explained.

In 1980's *Uprising* tour, Marley played for one million fans in six weeks. The Wailers attracted 100,000 Italians at a single show, and the audience waved Ethiopian flags. How strange is it that a country that forty-four years earlier had proudly attacked Ethiopia would now wave its free flag?

He ended the massive shows – 100,000 in Dublin, similar in London – with the acoustic "Redemption Song."

"'Redemption Song' is one of the most profound and important statements Bob ever uttered," said Neville Garrick, an artist who often collaborated with Marley for album covers and stage visuals.

"One of the most celebrated things Marcus Garvey ever said was, 'Up, ye mighty race: you can accomplish what you will.' To me, 'Redemption Song' is an update of that: it really lies with you; you have to make the move; you have to free your mind first before you can attain anything."

Marley learned he would die within weeks and decided to go out doing what he existed for: playing his music. At the last show, on September 23, 1980, in Pittsburgh, "Redemption Song" was one of the last songs he ever played live.

The final page of *Songs of Freedom* contains only the song's lyrics.

★ ★ ★

Marley's last days swirled in confusion as he tried to keep his fatal news private. In a homecoming of sorts, he converted to the Ethiopian Orthodox Church and was baptized under his African father's name as Berhane Selassie, the Christian Rasta. He descended into the Bavarian lowlands to seek eccentric cancer treatments, telling the wider world he had gone back to Ethiopia.

As spring coaxed a thaw out of the German mountains, Marley flew above them and across the vast ocean in a last run for home. He reached Miami, and, stranded on those shores, found himself redeemed into his father's land after a thirty-six-year sojourn on Earth.

Bob Marley once said to his wife, Rita, "I don't belong to anybody. I don't have a father on Earth. For me there is only the Father in heaven."

Marley left the Earth to seek his Father beyond life and death.

★ ★ ★

Bob Marley turned the suffering of his heart outward, used it to fuel his artistic ambitions, and to be more for others. He grew up with pain and changed it into healing for others.

We can see the extraordinary power of his songs on display in UFC Fight Night Glasgow: Bisping vs. Leites. Michael Bisping, England's greatest mixed martial artist, fought Thales Leites, an elite Brazilian, on home soil in July 2015. The arena went dark as the huge audience prepared to boo Leites on his walk to the cage.

And then Marley's "Three Little Birds" echoed through the arena. The British fans unthinkingly sang along as Leites smiled. What other artist could make 10,000 angry fans cheer the bad guy? "He's walking into hostile territory here, but he chose a walkout song that has the whole crowd singing along. I'm impressed," said commenter Brian Stann.

Some call it a twoness: being white and black, isolated from each world for not being black enough, not being white enough. But Marley found a way to make himself enough as a oneness: both a white man and a black man, a human, and he laid his unified body down as a bridge for us to cross.

Perhaps Marcus Garvey's great prophecy looked not to the near future, but to the deep past. Through Marley, Garvey tells us that Ethiopia reached out her hand and touched God.

And we know that thousands of years ago well before time, humanity rose above the animal kingdom, found a deeper life, and emerged from Ethiopia to spread over the world, touching the hand of God.

Ethiopia is the ancestral home of all humans. Look to Africa for the crowning of a black king. He shall be the redeemer.

But to see that, we must first emancipate ourselves from mental slavery. None but ourselves can free our minds. As Bob Marley says, Won't you help to sing these songs of freedom?

Epilogue

In May 2006, a man snuck up to the Black Loyalist Heritage Centre in Birchtown. The new museum held artifacts, names, and stories from Boston King and all the other Nova Scotians stolen from Africa and who brought themselves to this new place. The man used the darkness of the evening to close in on one of the two buildings. He set it on fire and retreated.

At 9:50 p.m., Everett Cromwell, a member of the Centre, found the treasure trove ablaze. "The railing was burning off and falling off, and it was just getting up under the eaves," he told Shunpiking.org.

Fire officials sped to the scene, but declared it a write-off. It was obviously arson. Police even said they knew who did it. But the officer who was supposed to be investigating it took a vacation instead, and nobody was ever charged.

Two months earlier, someone had thrown firebombs at the Black Cultural Centre outside of Dartmouth, so the possible connection struck many people. But police told Shunpiking.org straight away that neither of the two fire attacks had any racist motivation.

"We know that from the motive of the individual involved [in Birtchtown]. It was not race-related. Race was not [his] motive. Dartmouth was a different set of circumstances. And it was not race-related."

Police confidently told the people of Birchtown that they knew who the arsonist was, that he was white, and that his motivations were "personal." He was actually just burning the museum in revenge against one guy, who was black. The target of the attack had no involvement in the Centre. Locals told Shunpiking.org that police showed great sympathy and compassion to the alleged arsonist. But they never arrested him.

★ ★ ★

Beverly Cox, site manager for the museum, learned of the fire while she was on vacation in the Caribbean. She came home to rally her staff and volunteers. The community criss-crossed the province and raised $2.3 million in eighteen months. They spent years drafting plans, imagining a new centre, and finally opened it in 2015.

"The society took a long time to heal. They were really, really hurt. And it took a long time before people could even start coming back to this site. It was just so, so devastating that you started in 1989, and here it is 2006 and we've worked so hard, you have this little office we're so proud of, and next thing you know it's gone up in ashes," she told me as she showed me the new centre for a CBC radio documentary called *Remembering Nova Scotia's Black Loyalist History*.

Just a few metres from the pit house – a replica of the dug-out huts the Black Loyalists lived in during the early years – rises the impressive new museum. Cox explained that the physical design of the building recreates the Black Loyalist experience. You start walking a path between tall stone walls. You can't see where you're going.

"The entry is sort of symbolic with these stone walls. It symbolizes the door of no return. If somebody comes in through this entrance, and is following this stone wall, you really don't know where you're going to end up. But you also have on this stone wall a conversation between a descendent and an ancestor," Cox said.

Inside feels like a spacious mausoleum. Half the museum is a rock wall holding artifacts and interactive displays. It feels like it was carved out of a natural stone cropping.

But the roof is glass, and the far wall is glass. Half the floor is glass, too, offering a view into recreated archeological digs.

"It also speaks to our ancestors and standing on the shoulders of our ancestors as we walk along," Cox explained. "So we walk on their shoulders and that's where we are today. This beautiful building … we celebrate our ancestors and their journey and our history."

Light streams in through the hundreds of names etched in the glass wall. Behind her voice, you can hear water sloshing against a shore. Like a drum beat, it reminds you of those early refugees sailing for freedom.

"We talk about the first race riot in Canada, which happened here in Shelburne. It was about work and it was about their survival. White people weren't getting the jobs; they were giving them to black people because they didn't have to pay them as much. That caused unrest."

Some of that unrest continues. In October 2014, someone broke into the Centre while it was under construction and caused $20,000 in damage. Nobody was arrested.

But Cox is undaunted. She thinks the museum can make a difference in how Nova Scotians see their history. "I always say to people who visit here, we have a collective history. We're all immigrants to this country and we've all helped contribute to the building of our country. Your history is no more important than my history, but when you're able to talk about the collective history of our country, that's a good thing."

★ ★ ★

On a bright day in February 2010, the winter sun fell on thick, crusty snow. By noon, temperatures reached the daily high: -14 Celsius. Thrusts of wind dropped it to -24. Eddie Carvery lit a fire under a barrel and boiled a pot of water. He dropped a handful of spaghetti noodles into it and boiled lunch for himself and his dog Spike. The two camped on the edge of the Bedford Basin, straight in the path of the blasts of winter wind coming off the Atlantic. Eddie was bundled into a worn winter coat and toque.

A chain-link fence separated Eddie and Spike from Seaview dog park. Inside, four people huddled in the shrinking patches of sunlight and encouraged their dogs to run and poop. The dogs pooped where Eddie was born, where he was raised, where he watched in furious disgust as Halifax bulldozed his world house by house.

Halifax first officially discussed destroying Africville in 1915. City aldermen planned to write words on official paper that would turn one of Canada's oldest black communities into an industrial district. They'd figure out what industry to put there after the black people were gone. Already, Africville housed a prison, took the city's raw sewage, and would soon be the home of the city dump.

But the Great War dragged on, and the 1917 Halifax Explosion destroyed chunks of the city. Plans to destroy Africville were shelved in favour of plans to create a new North End.

The city resurrected the plans in the 1960s, this time plotting the destruction under the euphemism of urban renewal. Africvillians fought for the services their taxes paid for, but still walked unpaved roads and pumped water from a common well. They fought city hall and lost. People sold their houses to the city, or got swindled out of them by the city, and left. Bulldozers rumbled in like heavy-duty buzzards and ate the corpses of the empty houses. By the late 1960s, Africville looked like a war-bombed village. Everyone left by January 1970.

Eddie left, too, but stuck around. In the summer of 1970, he got hold of a tent and walked from north-end Halifax to Africville, a trip that takes about thirty minutes on foot. He was the only person in the pot-holed village until city crews arrived. They shot him odd looks as they hauled the ruins of the demolished buildings into the town dump and set them on fire.

Eddie spent the day thinking about the generations of his family that had fought to protect this village from the ever-sprawling city of Halifax just over the hill. He thought back to the Maroons who may have been the first black settlers here, living north of the city of Halifax in the 1790s and building its fortifications. That night, he decided not to go home. He decided he was home. He pitched his tent and slept in Africville.

Living a humble, monkish life in the ruins, he found a refuge from his chaotic existence in Halifax. Racists set his tent on fire, shot at him from the street, and the city stole his campers. He suffered eight heart attacks and came close to freezing to death too many times to remember.

On that frosty winter's day in 2010, he glanced at his latest trailer, on which he'd painted "Africville Protest." After feeding Spike his lunch, Eddie went into his trailer and tried to keep warm. "I can go days without eating and not realize how hungry I am until I do eat," he told me. I was there researching *The Hermit of Africville*, my biography of him that was published on the fortieth anniversary of his extraordinary protest.

"People want to let that segment of our society die. I'm not prepared to do that. It's our space – the black space. We earned it as Canadians," he said. "Our ancestors paid the price and today we are excluded from history. This is my life. This is my job. If I don't do it, I feel like I'm betraying myself and my purpose."

When he closed his eyes, he saw Africville alive. Walk through its old land with him and he'll tell you where Joe Skinner and his family lived. He'll tell you where he and his brother Victor went berry picking as boys. He'll show you where a police officer shot and killed his dog one day in his childhood. He'll show you the hungry ghost of the prison that ate so many of his friends and family.

But you won't see any bitterness. Eddie is a warm, intelligent man who passionately shares the lessons of forty years in the wilderness. He's a black Moses that nobody followed, so he went into the desert alone. At times, especially in the post-Christmas winter, depression floods him and threatens to sink him.

But he revives, and marches on. "What I went through out here, it was a transformation. I was stripped of everything I believed in, everything I thought was right, and then I had to reconnect my bones and put myself back together," he explained.

The scattered people of Africville built new lives in Halifax, or moved away. Eddie watched Halifax try to erase Africville from its history. Eddie refused to let that happen over his living body. No matter how many times he was forced out of Africville, he always returned. At night, he dreamed of Africville redeemed. In an alternative reality, the city invested in Africville, and in 2010 enjoyed a vibrant, wealthy, and cool urban village just over the hill.

But he awakes to see the same bleak winter landscape emptied of Africville.

"I see us being lost as a culture, as a people who contributed to Canada. It's evolved from being not just about Africville. It's about a space, a feeling toward a congregation in our community, and it's a black congregation, and it's where we're placed on the ladder in this society. We need to reform this society and include everybody. We're losing that space. Even though we're growing in population, we're shrinking in size of community, of space," he told me.

Fighting for Africville, for the black space, heated his heart with pride. It gave his life purpose and clarity. It brought him visitors from across the globe.

He saw the ideology of racism clearly, and saw that it was hollow junk. Being a black man in a white-dominated culture, he knew for a fact that it wasn't innate and inherited differences that hampered his people. He also knew he contained Mi'kmaq DNA from his mother's side of the family, and European DNA from his father's side of his family.

He knew personally how intelligent, talented, and hard-working Africvillians were. He saw clearly the mental chains that held people back so often, and how hard those who broke through had to work.

"I can see them fixing Africville and I can see them fixing the rest of the problems, because it's not our problem to inherit. Somebody did something wrong and they messed up our system. They gave us the face of a racist and we don't deserve it because we're Canadians and we're all colours," he said.

The ideology of racism worked itself deeply into the human consciousness and became an obvious truth, despite guarding a lie at its heart. There are no human races, just different cultures. There are no natural prisoners, no natural guards.

The European colonists of centuries past brought

the ideology to Mi'kma'ki and renamed the land New France, then Nova Scotia. But the old ideas rotted away the foundations, sprouted mildew in the walls, grew mold in the attic. The ideology of racism turned Canada into a sick country, coughing and spluttering, unwilling to heal itself.

"You're on the wrong horse. You're in the wrong country," Eddie said to those who brought racism to this land. "What you did was wrong when you brought those people here in slavery. What they did in servitude, they dug out them streets, they hold a position in this country called Canada. These people should have a role of prominence. We should pay homage and say, 'Wow, what a fascinating country we've got. These people gave it to us, they carved out the roads. Let's make this a beautiful history.'"

Where others see history as inherited and unalterable, Eddie sees a vivid, living part of our collective identity. We don't have to see ourselves as the people who brought slaves here – we can also see ourselves as the people who got free.

Mathieu Da Costa, Henri Membertou, and Samuel Champlain ate and drank together on the Fundy shores in 1605, dreaming of a new world of tolerance and diversity. Of prosperity and respect. They were the first Canadians.

Boston King bought the chains that were slipped around his infant ankle and built his freedom in Birchtown. He was a great Nova Scotian. Richard Preston galloped around the scattered black communities and created a collective identity. He was a great Nova Scotian. This land was so highly esteemed that Marcus Garvey visited to deliver the second great prophecy of his career. He told Nova Scotia first: We must emancipate ourselves from mental slavery. None but ourselves can free our minds.

Eddie Carvery reached the same conclusion in Africville on his long walk from Babylon to Zion

"This gives you pride that you feel deep down in your soul and makes you feel like you're going to last forever, because you've got a worth, you've got a value. That's what this protest has done for me. I was broke in the city. I was a broken man. I came to Africville. I prayed so hard, I was completely broke. I asked God to pick me up. I didn't want to be the liar I was when I walked out of the city. I was everything to everybody, but to myself, my own worst enemy," Eddie said.

"When I started fighting for Africville, it changed me. I stopped being the centre of attraction for me. I learned to put me far from Eddie.

"Since I been out here, I learned what discipline is, because you have to be very disciplined to be here. I've learned what it is to be patient. I realized how long a winter's night is, and the extent of the rain. Stuff that I never thought about, I've had time to think about."

Nova Scotia thought about it, too. Every summer, Eddie is joined by dozens of tents and campers, and hundreds of people as Africville's scattered children come home for a summer reunion. In 2008, 1,500 people from across the world came back to Africville. In 2010, the mayor of Halifax said what most black people knew to be true all along: the city was wrong to destroy Africville. Mayor Peter Kelly apologized.

"We realize words cannot undo what has been done, but we are profoundly sorry and apologize to all the former residents and their descendants," he said.

"You lost your houses, your church, all of the places where you gathered with family and friends to mark the milestones of your lives. For all that, we apologize.

"We apologize to the community elders, including those who did not live to see this day, for the pain and loss of dignity you experienced.

"We apologize to the generations who followed, for the deep wounds you have inherited and the way your lives were disrupted by the disappearance of your community.

"We apologize for the heartache experienced at the loss of the Seaview United Baptist Church, the spiritual heart of the community, removed in the middle of the night. We acknowledge the tremendous importance the church had, both for the congregation and the community as a whole.

"Let us today start to write the rest of our story together."

In 2012, the city finally made good on a twenty-year-old promise and built a replica of Africville's church. They built it on Eddie's protest site, evicting him once more in the process. Eddie moved down by the water and kept the protest flame burning. He'll stay there until everyone – all Canadians, regardless of colour – can see how beautiful Africville was, can see it for the flowers, and can start to see our history as not one thin white line to the past, but a thick rope cording together all of our histories.

Eddie won't stop until everyone feels that same

deep pride in the heart that makes you realize why Canada is a country worth fighting for, and worth celebrating. Until Africville is redeemed. Until our collective African roots are redeemed.

★ ★ ★

Hundreds of black-hearted children gather each year in Glace Bay on August 15. Adults, too, come to celebrate Marcus Garvey's birthday. The centre of celebrations is the UNIA Hall – the only UNIA Hall still standing in all of Canada. Marcus Garvey Days give locals three days of dance, history, and business lessons in the great man's shadow.

"It's a place for blacks to come and learn about themselves," Theresa Brewster told me in 2009. She's the chair of the UNIA and spent years resurrecting the hall and rescuing it from slow collapse. She brought it back to life. Her mother was white and her father black, so according to UNIA rules at the time of Garvey's visit, she couldn't have held office. She couldn't have saved the hall.

But she did, and black-hearted people of many skin colours thank her for it.

In 2014, the UNIA celebrated its one hundredth anniversary. Glace Bay held a double party for Marcus Garvey's birthday, and for that of the organization he birthed. The local radio station covered the event and unintentionally showed the need for education. It told listeners that Garvey was "a journalist from England who moved to Glace Bay in the 1920s" to establish the "first Universal Negro Improvement Association" in Canada. Well, some of those words could be organized into the truth.

"Marcus Garvey was their salvation," Theresa Brewster told a reporter that summer. "He tried very hard to get blacks together to own their own businesses, their own homes. Education was the most important thing."

Today, the UNIA Hall he inspired continues to inspire others.

"It's a place for blacks to come and learn about themselves," she said. "I think what we've accomplished is that these kids are all different shades, and they see their blackness in their heart. A lot of the kids didn't know there were other kids like themselves. They're proud now."

Acknowledgements

Eddie Carvery welcomed me into his Africville protest trailer and spent years teaching me about racism and resistance as we wrote *The Hermit of Africville*. He planted the seeds; this is the flowering.

Paul O'Connell, my editor at *The Chronicle Herald*, published a 2009 article on the Nova Scotia roots of "Redemption Song" – this builds on that. Steven Laffoley, my friend and fellow writer, suggested that article would make a good book. He texted me a few times a year to remind me I should write that book. Thanks, Steven – here it is!

Lesley Choyce, publisher of Pottersfield Press, embraced the idea in its infancy and grew it into adulthood. My editors Peggy Amirault and Julia Swan corrected away many mistakes and improved the writing.

My parents, Gail and Jack Tattrie, gave me the heart to climb the mountain and see the vision of Marcus Garvey and Bob Marley. The writer Giselle Melanson Tattrie helped me develop the themes in this book, and also lets me be her husband.